Catch Your Breath, Find Y(
4 Psychological & Bib...

4 BREATHS

Keith Hughes, M.A.

contact info:
    www.keithcounseling.com
    keith@keithcounseling.com
    Instagram: Keithcounsel

4 Breaths
Copyright © 2024 by **Keith Hughes, M.A.**

All rights reserved. No part of this book may be reproduced or transmitted in any form or by any means, electronic or mechanical, including photocopying, recording, or by any information storage and retrieval system, without permission in writing from the copyright owner.

This book was printed in the United States of America.

Editors:
Carla Davis
Ross Wesley Harris

Book Cover Design and Interior Formatting by 100Covers.

Thank you to My Heart Keepers:
    Lord and Savior Jesus Christ
    My wife Marie
    Sons Eliseo and Enrique
    Mom & Dad (Patty & Kenny)
    Billy Hughes "I take your bullet, you'll take mine"

Thought & Spiritual Mentors:
    The Apostle Paul
    Jim Griffin
    Dr. Harl Hargett
    Dr. Arlene Martinez Meads
    Dr. Jordan Peterson
    Fr. Richard Rohr
    Timothy Keller
    N.T. Wright
    Pastor Tim Mackey

Other Influencers and Inspiration:
    To all my clients I've worked with over the years, I thank you for the privilege of serving you
    Lost & Found Inc.
    Bono
    Jimmy Connors
    Deanna Farrugia
    Jeff Meythaler
    Mason Moore
    Brad Heykoop
    Pastor Nick Lilo
    Pastor Larry Renoe
    'Stupid Galatians' Small Group
    Waterstone Community Church
    Grace Bible Church
    Grace Mountain Church
    Passion Play of Denver

CONTENTS

Introduction v

All That You Can't Leave Behind 1
Rarely Are Things As They Seem 27
The Worship Code 55
Mashalem "It Is Finished" Part I 73
Mashalem "It Is Finished" Part II 97

References 111

INTRODUCTION

*Every morning I wake up and I ask myself
"what breath do I need today? Thank you Keith!"*
—**Deanna Farrugia Leader Coach**

FIND YOUR LIFE. In order to find your life, catching your breath is essential. There are things in life that take your breath (life) away or give you breath (life). Thank you for your gracious attention. It is my earnest desire to figure out how to encapsulate and/or conceptualize what I've learned over 35 years being a therapist. These are central lessons for mental and spiritual health. I hope to articulate and share with you my thoughts so they might encourage you, bring new ideas to mind and maybe practice them for the nourishment of your life. Although I am with a perplexed mind that I would dare to add toward the ocean of "self-help/self-development" book shelves, but I think the 25,000 hours of direct clinical work with people, is enough clinical observation to substantiate my sharing with you on these ideas. After long bouts with doubt authoring this book, I cannot deny the urge to honor my mentors, teachers, clients and peers who have all shaped this content and urged for this content to be brought to light.

To begin with, I think we would naturally agree it is of great value to discover new elements that add breath and oxygen to our life. By "oxygen" I mean how we find renewed energy, toward our life in general or something specific. And the things that give us "oxygen" for this books purpose, I am calling "breath". Life has a way of taking your breath away. Whether that's through excitement, overwhelmed beauty, or horrific tragedy. It can literally take your breath away. It is such a thing, our breath. Without the ability to breathe, we die. I know sounds so simple, even trite. But as we stop and consider this for a minute, while we sit and breathe realizing life is made up of breath, uncountable breaths. Without oxygen, we die. It never stops to confound me how important and critical things which we cannot see with the naked eye, can sustain our life or take away our life. Breath, wind, profound forces in the world I believe we take for granted. If you finish reading this book and feel like you gained some oxygen in your life, meaning, a new gained perspective, insight, encouragement and understanding, then I have done my job. Lack of oxygen in our blood and brain we begin to deteriorate in many ways; we become anxious, tired and compromised. Oxygen. Breath. Life. Synonyms. The title 4 breaths is my offering to describe the 4 essential psychological and biblical principles to infuse a flourishing life. These 4 breaths are available so that we understand, implement, manage and utilize so that we don't lose breath in life, not living optimally. If you can take these principles in deeply, I assure you that living will be full of breath, life, and oxygen.

In my counseling work with people I had begun somewhere in the last 5 years taking notice of some patterned responses of "breath" people were getting from counseling. Meaning, I started identifying with my clients what things were present in their lives that were sucking the life / 'breath' out of them. And conversely, I began to present the antidote to that loss of breath by offering how to find more breath in life. There started to emerge some noticeable entities that did either bring breath or loss of breath. As this was occurring, one Sunday morning in church, we (my wife and I) were listening to Pastor Nick Lillo preach on "the Ruach" of God. As he was teaching the meaning and use of God's "Ruach" my mind started to race in deep thought to what I experience in my work on a daily basis. I interact with people on a daily basis losing their breath in life and desperately trying to find it, and get it back. Ruach of God is simply the "Breath of God" and it is also interpreted as the "spirit" of God. In the New Testament, "spirit" in the Greek is "Pneuma". But Ruach is a Hebrew word for "breath". I was going to Title the book as 'Ruach" but I could already hear the push back from my peers, "so good luck marketing a book on a word most people have never heard nor can pronounce" . Nonetheless, Ruach is such a great word and a worthwhile study in the scriptures in how it is used. The Ruach of God is what he uses to create life. In Genesis we see God breathed "Ruach" life, water, mist, light into existence. The Ruach of God creates life! I started making the connection to God's Ruach. His breath creates life. We are made by his breath. Our own breath is essential and critical to living; and as we live we get to and need to find our breath in the life we lead. Further, we are constantly challenged in contending with the things trying to take our breath away.

Fundamentally, compromised mental health can simply be understood when an individual loses their self- awareness. Once we lose self-awareness we lose our ability to discern our life. We are usually lost in a state of being that causes us to cross over others boundaries, fall into deep states of anxiety and despair, lose perspective, and cling onto the destructive outlet. Versus the sustaining outlets life has to offer. Keeping self-awareness can be a tricky thing. It isn't like we wake up one day and lose our awareness, it's an undercurrent we can slide into that can take us out into the depths of darkened places.

One of those breaths has to deal with finding new perspective. Life, full of all types of malevolence, evil, tragedies, and just the daily mishaps certainly keeps switching the lenses on us causing us to lose perspective. And when I say 'lose perspective' I simply mean as life hits, how we are caused to see ourselves and our situation that might take away from us the ability to see life in a way that it can work for us. The clinical term is called reframing. To put it simply, when disruption, pain, tragedy hits, it seems to then say, "I can't do this", "I am overwhelmed" or this "is a total curse". But that's not true. Reframing helps us find a new lens on things so we might find 'the way' and even the 'the gift' of what has just occurred. Perspective is found by learning the skill of reframing. Countless times in my work I hear, "ahhh, that makes sense now. I have never seen it or heard it put that way, but I can now breathe and move forward now". By being able to reframe ones dilemma, situation or event, we get to find a perspective that we can live or work with causing us to have more life/ breath about the situation. So I find reframing an essential breath to find.

We lose ourselves when good things become ultimate thigs. This breath is in regards to what we place too much reliance and meaning on things that will not sustain us. This would be the breath called the Code of Worship. We will look into how much the act of worship is a part of our culture, how it's within our DNA to centralize the "good" things of life and make them "ultimate". And by doing so, it is the set up for chaos and suffering to occur. And to take things a step further, this chapter explores what drives us to worship or 'centralize' the wrong things in life by looking at our core desires and how desires get disordered which influences our choices and behaviors. Dealing with the heart so that we can set our desires in order as best we can. We look into adapting strategies that keep our desires fulfilled in some kind of orderly fashion. We become what we worship.

What we hold onto in life has much to do about the breath we take in how we can forgive others and ourselves. Looking at this via the metaphor of travelling and how much we decide to carry in our limited suitcase of life. What we choose and how much we choose to pack in our suitcase affects our travels. Suitcases full of resentments, criticisms, anger, and shame tend to limit our ability to travel well in life. What we choose to hold onto in our hearts makes all the difference in how we relate to the world. Being able to figure out forgiveness is a way we gain and give breath in life.

The final breath contends with our sin, "falling down", our brokenness, our shame. And the way by which we can find breath is through the understanding of The Cross. More specifically, it is the understanding of the final words of Jesus on the cross, "it is finished" (Mashalem). There are multiple and layered messages to unpack from the Cross that can assist us in how we contend with our own decline or falling down resulting in guilt and shame. Guilt and shame might very well lead the pack of afflictions to the soul. The cancer of the soul. Certainly, shame takes our breath away. Jesus on the cross gives us much to consider and internalize in regard to pain, suffering, shame, grace, love, and forgiveness. In this chapter I present a covert confession and an 'ask' that comes from the Cross that I hope gives you life.

The 4 breaths. Take them in and let them out, and then we know how might we live. The practice of breathing is an important one. When we take time to practice deep breathing, we find our life, we find the moment, and we are here. We are living. Find your breath, you find your life. If you know how to reframe and find perspective, keep the ultimate, ultimate; forgive the wound that's not serving your soul well, allow the Cross to speak the power of 'it is finished'. The power of our guilt and shame is over and we can walk on, breathing in Spirit, breathing Spirit between one another.

ALL THAT YOU CAN'T LEAVE BEHIND

Breath of Forgiveness

"Love is not the easy thing
The only baggage you can bring
Is all that you can't leave behind"
—U2

"AND THE VERDICT is, not guilty!" A gut punch. A pause to the heart. Their oxygen left their soul, their bodies, and their mouth. Gasping for life. The family who lost their beloved son and brother who was murdered by a shot in the back, watched in disbelief as the alleged offender was not convicted of murder 1. Trying to gather themselves in some kind of manner was an act of sheer survival. Trying to fight off feeling violated one more time seemed nearly impossible. The family members did the best they could to comfort themselves as they lingered in the cold and empty courthouse halls. Not wanting to leave but yet hardly standing to stay, slowly they part and move onward to their next destination.

Sister of the victim, Alisha, in a daze, finds the elevator, trusting it's the right one to descend her toward the parking garage. She waits, elevator opens, and enters, pressing the button for the ground level. Making the descent, naturally, there is a pause, and doors open, allowing another passenger onto the elevator. Proceed to descend, and pause, doors open for the next floor. This is the longest elevator ride. Still staring down at the ground in disbelief. Alisha stands, and others shuffle as the last passenger enters the elevator. The tight quarters only escalate her sense of life crashing in on her, she is just trying to get out and to her car.

The door closes, yet still staring downward, a glance up and over, eyes focused and in sheer disbelief, she has to do the acrobatics of belief versus disbelief of who is standing beside her. The man who she believes and knows murdered her brother, found not guilty, is standing right next to her. He stares straight ahead, smug and still. A wave of heat, rage, fear, and a thousand thoughts crossed her mind of what she could and would do to this man. She is sweating. Shoulders, neck, and arms tense and it is fight or flight on steroids. "Justice! Where are You?! Or shall I bring it here?" These are the thoughts going through her mind. The elevator ride is an eternity. She is near certain that the rest of the elevator car can hear her heart pounding and hear her breathing as loud as the elevator cables. "I can kill him. I can make this right. No. Yes. No!"

The elevator stops. Doors open, and people exit one by one. The man next to her exits, and Alisha follows. She walks behind him in exact step with his. She stops. He continues. Staring at him from behind, just like he stood behind her brother before shooting and killing him. Alisha had revenge at her access. She finds herself in that moment, able to imitate the act committed against her brother. But something came upon her. A drastic shift. Her heart broke. Sweating in sheer exhilaration she yells, "Hey! Stop!" The man stops, startled, turns around. Looks right at Alisha, shaded fear in his eyes. "Do you know who I am?" she asks. He nods, quietly. Affirming who she is and what is happening here. Now I know Alisha, personally, and I know she is capable of her own malevolence. No stranger to aggression and settling the score. Alisha makes the walk toward him. Stops before him. Staring at him, cold, hard stare. Long pregnant pause. Then, heavy surrendering arms open, she leans toward him, and she embraces him, arms around him, holding the murderer, crying. "I forgive you. Go in peace". At that moment, feeling like her heart was pounding out of her body, but it was the rage and hatred that was leaving her, and it was the grace and forgiveness that was being poured onto her brother's murderer. She was free. And maybe so was he.

I know at times it's a hard thing to find your breath. Alisha got her breath back and preserved it from being taken by rage and revenge. And she gave breath to the one who also needed it desperately. He was technically set free by the legal system but was offered another kind of freedom from the breath of forgiveness from Alisha.

When I refer to finding your breath, I mean to find life amidst a culture where the oxygen is often getting sucked out of the room by polarized beliefs, entitlement, political divisiveness, false ideologies shoved at you, or run the risk of being a victim to 'cancel culture'. The cancel culture that prowls in this present time dares to cancel individuals in some sort of leadership position who have either said something, implied something, did an unwelcomed act years ago, or just may have stood up for something that this group dislikes and will cancel you / fire you from your post.

In other words, this current cultural climate is the antidote to forgiveness. It is quick to cancel rather than trying to learn and understand what and why you may have said/done umpteen years ago. You just get cancelled. It's like, who cares if you have changed? Who cares that there may have been a contextual component to your behavior? We do not care. That does not fit with our ideology now. And so you are canceled. Being canceled is a way culture attempts to take one's breath away.

To me there seems to be a short list of critical decisions. Specifically, we are presented with 5 specific choices that greatly affect the trajectory of our path in life:

1. Who you marry.
2. Having or not having children.
3. What career you choose.
4. Whether or not you believe in God.
5. What or who you choose to forgive or not forgive.

Why forgiveness is considered to be one of the breaths of life is because NOT taking that breath of forgiveness toward ourselves or others holds long-lasting consequences on our mental health, physical health, quality of our social life, and spiritual fitness. The presence or absence of forgiveness determines a life with the weight of harbored anger, resentment and hurt. And those feelings take on a certain presence in our souls that shapes, colors and influences how we move toward, away from, or about people.

Forgiveness can make a difference in being fit physically, mentally, and emotionally. Otherwise, you become bankrupt both emotionally and psychologically. Forgiving is what brings oxygen into your soul and into the souls of others. Forgiveness is a two-way transaction. Forgiving another person actually makes them a better person, and improves the condition of our soul. Forgiveness truly is a lot like breathing. When we inhale forgiveness, being from others and/or God… it fills the lungs of our soul with life; and when we offer forgiveness to our transgressors it gives the oxygen, life, to them and releases from our soul's lungs the carbon dioxide—anger, resentment… It is reported that in assessing all of Jesus's teachings, approximately two-thirds of them were about or had to deal with forgiveness.

Throughout our life, we are constantly in the check and balance of what we must carry and hold on to, or what we should be letting go. The subtitle of this chapter "All that you can't leave behind" is a clever U2 lyric from the song, "Walk On" and the Title of their album "All That You Can't Leave Behind"(2000 U2). The album cover art also captures the band standing in the middle of an airport, painting the message of them as travelers reflecting upon what they must carry and what they must let go.

The drastically often used expression that "life is a journey" (one I have grown weary of) gives us the metaphor of life as something we travel through. Urging us to imagine as if we are travelers through time/life. However, I cannot argue, it certainly seems true enough, that we are traveling through stages, events, seasons, and current circumstances. We travel through, over, and around so much. And as we travel, there are things that occur. And things we gather along the way.

Travelers pick up items along the way in life that we deem necessary to hold on to: a memoir, a souvenir, even if just a photo. And as we gather things in life, at some point along the way we have to examine whether what we are holding on to is sustainable. Do I still have room for what I hold on to? Is what I am holding on to serving me well over a longer period of time? Our suitcase is limited in its capacity which suggests maybe we should be wise in how much we hold onto and cannot leave behind.

What is essential for us to hold onto? Is it worth it to keep adding to our luggage causing our travels to be bogged down by extra weight, tiring us to the point of exhaustion? Obviously, no. This metaphor works well in the actual sense of traveling. And I think it serves us in the figurative as well. Meaning, we get to decide what we get to 'hold onto' or items that cannot be left behind as: resentments, unforgiveness, grace, love, understanding, hatred, fears, memories, etc. Our capacity to hold onto things might be grand, but because we have large suitcases, does not mean it's wise to keep it them full. And there is a limit to the capacity of our luggage.

This brings up how we discern what we hold onto, which makes all the difference in how we travel. Though our wounds are full of meaning and memory, what we decide to hold onto from them deserves our attention. We are confronted with how do we hold on to or let go of those resentments, hurts, and anger. In other words, "Will I or won't I forgive?" Does my un-forgiveness (holding on) serve my travels? Maybe. Or is it making life harder to travel? Each of these options has it is own consequence. The one forgiving pays by letting go of their entitled emotions and power over their transgressor. It costs the one forgiving this kind of power. Not to forgive costs a soul a hefty charge. Deeply infused with a volume of anger, hatred or resentment decreases the ability of understanding, and we deny the soothing effect of compassion.

We have, at one point in our lives, experienced someone wronging us; offending us and hurting us, in some form or another. And we have, conversely, wronged, offended, or hurt someone in our life. And it becomes equally hard to reconcile the heart for both those situations. The pain of being hurt by another and/or the pain of knowing we hurt another has a significant impact forgiveness. And, if left unattended, our life/ soul/ mental health condition can at least be compromised or greatly impacted. How we overcome such hurt takes much work. The address of the transgression/ betrayal, the need for responsibility, and boundary realignment, and ultimately how does forgiveness come into play?

We all at some point hold onto things; things that really may not hold great eternal/long-term purpose. When I say "things", I mean feelings and actions from ways people have treated us in some dishonorable fashion. Or how "life" may have treated us. We hold onto those feelings such as resentment, anger, and disappointment for long and enduring periods and for some, a lifetime.

Why do we do this? I hope to answer this question momentarily, but first I want to introduce the topic of Forgiveness and unforgiveness. As a therapist for approximately 30 years, one of the central themes that comes up in my clinical work is the issue of forgiveness. When we sit down and start talking about the current circumstance or presenting problem; depression, anxiety, guilt, poor patterns of sabotage and failure; pervasive strains of mistrust; it isn't too long in the therapy journey before we uncover that the individual comes face to face with the reality of either needing to forgive, OR needing to *be* forgiven by someone /themselves.

Forgiveness, I find, is one of the central themes in mental health and spiritual fitness. Further, what winds up happening is the very idea and the act of forgiving presents a difficult challenge. It is rarely as easy to just say the phrase, "I forgive you" and forgiveness to take place. It can be extremely difficult and complicated; to forgive or be forgiven. Therefore, I intend to help you understand this concept and provide applicable ways to handle forgiveness. I desire to be sensitive to the deeper underpinnings and impact of forgiveness because it demands careful handling. I do not approach it as a religious demand which you may have seen it presented as. Yet, it is of high admonishment we consider forgiveness (self and others) because it will come down to affecting whether you are breathing in life or suffocating.

What Forgiveness IS

I read a beautiful description of forgiveness by Fr. Rohr from "The Wisdom Pattern".

"Forgiveness is probably the only human action that reveals three goodnesses simultaneously. When we forgive, we choose the goodness of the person over their faults, we experience Gods goodness flowing through ourselves, and we also experience our own goodness in a way that surprises us. (2020. *The Wisdom Pattern: Order, Disorder, Reorder*)

"The first 'goodness' is what particularly strikes me. 'Choose the goodness of the person over their faults.' This is packed with such deep principles for us to consider. One, choosing the goodness of a person is powerful because here we get to choose, trust, and call out, the goodness in someone who may have wronged us in some enormous way. Second, by choosing one's goodness over their faults, we attempt to help that other person be valued in light of their fault, transgression or sin. Like we witness with Jesus, forgiving others is a transcendent act that can help another be better. We help inform the other that by offering forgiveness, their soul is above their faults, that you see something better. And lastly, by choosing goodness over ones faults it helps point the other to a higher calling. It says, "I see there is good inside you so go and act out your goodness. Your fault is not held against you." Great principles I wanted to share as we go further into the definition of forgiveness and understanding how it works.

Forgiveness: by definition: To cease to feel resentment against (an offender): pardon, forgive one's enemies. 2a: to give up resentment of or claim to requital (see requital sense 1) tor forgive an insult. b: to grant relief from payment or debt—(Webster Dictionary2023). I try to simply define it as, *No longer hold against*. Before I outline the multitude attributes of forgiveness, and what it is and is not, it would be disingenuous to not predicate this with the appropriate context.

There are three dimensions we work from when we are confronted with the idea of forgiving. One dimension affords us the situation when the one who has wronged us is present, accessible and engaged with us to work out forgiveness. And further, this individual may also be seeking your forgiveness. As a result, the process and act of forgiveness presents itself to us, to engage or not.

The second dimension, and often tragic one, is forgiving when the transgressor is not accessible, unwilling to be contacted, gone. As a result, we are left with trying to figure out forgiveness on our own. Painfully difficult. As I mentioned at the start, it's a certain tragedy to try and figure out how to let go on your own.

And finally, the third dimension of forgiveness is the forgiveness we offer ourselves. Probably, the most problematic. I can honestly report that the struggle to forgive one's self is challenge that shows up in my office on a nearly daily basis. Forgiving ourselves is a heavy lift to make. And some would admit, the hardest of all. Feels like a literal mountain to move. And it really can be and is necessarily impossible.

The acceptance of our transgression is one thing. But to pardon and let go of self-hatred/anger takes an act of God it seems. Well, it did take an act of God. To quote the wisdom friend/mentor/teacher/hippy pastor, Jim Griffin, "you cannot give what you don't have". How can I forgive myself and others if I don't have any to offer? Makes too much sense.

This is a very important and poignant dimension for us to look into. What might life be like if we never heard or experienced forgiveness from another? What if you never had the understanding you were forgiven by something bigger than who you are? There seems, in my view, an existential, cosmic, spiritual understanding that we are longing to know we are at peace with the being, the universe, and God. Not knowing, an acceptance or reception of divine forgiveness, keeps a soul unsettled.

Imagine for a minute, embracing something immensely larger than you extending forgiveness and complete pardon. The "TETELESTAI"!!! "It is finished!! Imagine God saying, "I forgive you, the offense is gone, because I take the blame, I want you with me. You need me with you. No matter what, I forgive you. My forgiveness is yours forever. I know you are not perfect. I don't need you perfect. I want you to give me your shame, regret, anger, guilt, and sorrow. I know you cannot have all the right answers. I know you have this habit that's hard to break that you promised to stop. I heard every promise you broke. I know the words you spoke were so laced with hate. I understand your passion takes over and is uncontrollable sometimes. I see what goes on in the dark. I know you hate, and regret, and want what is so bad for you. I know you want that poison. I know you want to kill, and destroy, and I know you never meant it to go that far. All I can say is I love you, still. Please come here, I was wrong for you…I was nailed to a cross and bled over your sin, every single one of them and became every sin you commit. So, will you stay and accept my forgiving heart?" What if that lives in you?

Fight with malevolence

What may not be obvious at first is the correlation that seems to exist between forgiveness and malevolence. With the exception of the obvious malevolence that may occur toward us or what we may afflict on another. The initial confrontation we face is what to do when we have been wronged? Being wrecked and betrayed is no easy matter to recover from. And such experiences shape how we might view the world and ourselves. The second impact of experiencing hurt in the world is what we do with the wound? Untended hurt tends to create a certain internal belief and emotional atmosphere that lends to a skeptical and worse, cynical disposition. We all have at least had our drinks of cynicism. It certainly avails itself as a perceived defense against the world and such betrayal or hurt to happen again. But research has shown the opposite, that cynicism does not serve us well in the long game. It rather seems to lend the chance that it invites more malevolence or worse, assists in our chance to one day deliver it to others: even the score.

Instead, we are dared to take on the opposite approach and we figure out a way to let go of the anger, and the toxicity of what has occurred. We figure out how we recover so we can face the world open-armed, with a daring heart and holding out for what might be better people. In contrast, taking on this: 'people are mean, the world is dark, and I am looking out just for me, and it's just going to happen again'.

Fighting malevolence is a damn war we are confronted by, or we avoid. It calls me back to how the apostle Paul admonishes the church in his heed. "We wrestle not against flesh and blood but things unseen, spiritual wickedness and principalities in high places." I know that verse is often referenced to fighting spiritual entities (demons), but to understand it as just that, we miss the deeper idea Paul is trying to make. He did not say, "We are fighting demons and ghosts". Principalities and unseen entities may also lend to the war we have inside of us contending with our 'demons' of our own malevolence, anger, bitterness, resentment, fear, and hatred. We wrestle with the things in our hearts that are attempting to shape and influence our very core.

When I present the interpretation of that verse in that manner, I sometimes get pushback that I am being naïve and just don't 'get it', that evil and the devil are at work trying to bring us down. And I completely understand the position. Yes, there are demons in this world. Certainly, the realm of spirit has been understood and acknowledged for thousands of years. I am even willing to not contest the stance because I have realized that this is a way we fight against the things coming against us. If one wants to attach it to the devil, it's a construct that makes sense to people.

What matters in the end is we are fighting against evil, not allowing it to rob us of optimism, hope and love. I can agree, evil and all it is attached to and what it encompasses is something we will contend with. We need to stay awake of its presence. More importantly not to allow it take residence in us. Therefore, we must take note that there is a fight and it's usually within us as well as outside us. The following are more attributes that comprise or are related to forgiveness which I find noteworthy.

Anger: Forgiveness is directly correlated with our contention with anger. Whether it is us or transgression by someone else, anger is the emotion we are trying to resolve. By forgiving ourselves or someone, it is our attempt to let go and resolve the anger. Anger can be a difficult emotion to resolve. It acts as a protector, defense from further hurt. Holding onto it can feel like a sense of power and even control. Therefore, forgiving it can make us feel very vulnerable because it requires us to let go of that power and open ourselves up to potentially be hurt again. But by forgiving we are actually taking on the "true power" position. And that is the next thing forgiveness "is".

True Power: True vs False power. This is a dilemma throughout the world. The pursuit of power. But what kind of power is hard to discern. As humans, we often get seduced into thinking that force, aggression, being right, winning, wealth is real power. I think we all know the consequences of pursuing that sort of finite power. Forgiveness is true power simply because our forgiving another is the act of restoring another person who has wronged you, and it calls them back into order and toward potentially being a better human being. Forgiving empowers them while also helping you no longer becoming toxic from anger and resentment. It is always most powerful to lift up others, especially the ones hurting you. "Forgive them, they know not what they do". Christ forgiving his killers. The power to exercise forgiveness is our defiance against malevolence. Protesting against the force of anger, bitterness so we do not become the thing that betrayed or wounded us.

Decision: Forgiveness is a decision, and most likely a thousand decisions to help us change our mind about someone or something.

Release: Forgiveness is a releasing of your feelings and thoughts about someone/something

Humbling: By forgiving it addresses the idea that by NOT forgiving, you are better than the other person who wronged you.

A surrender: Forgiveness is an act, a choice and an obligation for our better self. "Each time you offer a surrender, each time you trust the dying, your faith is led to a deeper level, and you discover your true self – the Christ in you". Richard Rohr

For both parties: Forgiveness is for the betterment of both the forgiver and the one needing forgiveness

Heroism: When we forgive another, we are helping another person become restored, put back together hopefully for the good. By forgiving, we help the other person have a chance to be less tormented by their guilt and anguish thus you act as a hero for them. And you get to save yourself from possible mental and emotional hell. It's a peculiar thing we decide to do when we choose our embrace with anger versus forgiveness toward another.

Payment: It's not always described in this manner, but forgiving is a payment you make. But you get to choose which kind of payment to make. Not forgiving creates a certain kind of payment, I will elaborate on later. Forgiveness is a payment we make because when we do, we are sacrificing our perceived right to be angry and owed; sacrifice our perceived power. Letting go is our down **payment on our freedom.**

Dismissal: It's a dismissal of a wrong, putting life back in order. No longer holding it against the other person /self.

Heal: Forgiveness is a way we heal; both by receiving and giving

Breath: As described in the introduction, forgiveness in our life is a breath we need to have and one we get to offer. Receiving forgiveness from God and others breathes into the heart the hope that we have another chance; we are not held in contempt; we are given the room to be good in one another's eyes. Giving the breath of forgiveness affords a breath toward anther and also for yourself. The letting go of that anger or whatever, now just opened up more room in your heart and soul for life and love to live. You are offering oxygen to the other and yourself at the same time. And lastly, when we forgive ourselves, we admit so many things. We admit that we're not what we believed we were and are culpable of such fallen behavior. When we forgive ourselves, it's our moment we are taking a deep breath in and out, so that we might live.

What Is Not Forgiveness

A Feeling: In my counseling work, one of the barriers to forgiveness I have come upon is forgiveness is perceived as being a part of or attached to some kind of emotion. I may hear, "I don't know I just am waiting to feel like forgiving him/her". Forgiveness may be associated with or supported by certain emotions like compassion, love, inspiration, etc. Forgiveness is not conditioned or reliant upon those emotions to offer it or receive it. And by itself, forgiveness is not a feeling. It is a verb and a noun. Forgiveness is not an emotion. I want us to consider that the act of forgiveness may promote certain profound emotions, but it is not an emotion.

Condoning: Another and often confusing barrier to forgiveness is that, to the heart, condoning tends to feel like if it lets go and forgives, it somehow condones/agrees with the transgressed behavior. Again, vulnerability is a challenge in forgiveness, opening up to potential hurt. Forgiveness is not condoning, it is pardoning the offense and letting go of holding it against the person while still acknowledging the behavior was 'wrong'.

Reconciliation: Forgiving another person does not necessarily mean you have to reconcile with them. It is sometimes confusing for us to forgive another person who has deeply hurt or violated us, because to forgive might suggest that we are now reconciled and back in a relationship with them. This is not true. Forgiveness can help in the reconciling of a relationship. But it is also possible to forgive that person but due to personal needs for emotional, psychological, and physical safety, it is wise not to be nearby or in a relationship with them. You can forgive your ex-spouse but not stay with them. We can forgive so that we can care for our souls and seek peace.

Magic word: One of the schemes of avoiding the true work of forgiveness is the old "sweep it under the rug". And how we do this is by the psychological acrobatics of once we are hurt, mad, or offended we try to shrink down the size of the act/behavior and the feelings to where we try not to make it mean anything so we can avoid the hard work of forgiveness. Forgiveness requires addressing feelings, actions, explanation, payments, sacrifice, discovery and all those have levels of uncertainty. So, instead of contending with all the hard work, we tend to do what may be called "cheap forgiveness" and say, "I forgive you, and let's move on". Or even more, we just say it in our minds, "It is ok, if I don't forgive, it is not a big deal", meanwhile hurt, resentment, anger grows. Forgiveness is not a magic word, but when hearing it, it certainly can be quite healing. However, the one saying "I forgive" without full understanding and engaging in the process of forgiveness may still entrap us in anger and withholding. Forgiveness is a magical process, not a magical word. It's a magical decision that demands awareness.

Being weak or co-dependent: Forgiving someone is not a sign you are being weak or a form of co-dependence. It's worth repeating, forgiving another is vulnerable and feels like a surrender. Yet, do not be deceived, vulnerability is strength, not weakness. It's a different kind of boldness. It's an incredible act of power to forgive. What it really does, is it offers another person emotional, spiritual, and psychological freedom. Forgiveness also takes a lot of strength to decide not to hold onto the illusive power of anger and replace it with peace. To empower another person with forgiveness might be one of the most impactful and powerful things you can do. We don't recognize much how humility is a force that changes lives. Culturally, our perception and pictures of strength tend to be myopic. So, forgiveness is not weak, rather it's heroic.

Religion and Forgiveness

It is a difficult thing to distinguish if religion has helped or hindered the understanding of forgiveness. Honestly, I have seen it do both. In short, it has been observed that religion, in some circles, makes forgiveness a command to just do in order to excuse a transgression but while holding on to the anger and resentment. Even though religion may have muddied the waters about the idea and purpose of forgiveness, I do think that ultimately its intent is good, as it is often encouraged by church/religion to go ahead, you should forgive.

The way I have seen religion hinder the power of true forgiveness is how it has presented it as an empty command and obligation. A moral act that should just be done. Which, in all intent and purposes, yes, forgive! But it comes with great consequence whenever we do things without deeper understanding. Dangerous to do something that you do not understand. To just forgive because one is required to do so is as disingenuous as giving an expensive gift to a distant and unknown relative, simply because there is blood relation.

Doing things without understanding stands too close to superstition, as far as I am concerned. A forced act in the name of God. As a result, only leaving people more embittered. However, with that, religion is reading and acting in accordance with what is certainly instructed by God and His teachers. Amongst many other things forgiveness is exalted and admonished in Christianity with high importance, probably right there with love.

I think the most popular charge comes from Jesus. When he is asked, "Lord, how often shall my brother sin against me and I forgive him? Up to seven times?" Jesus said to him, "I do not say to you, up to seven times, but up to seventy times seven." It is probably fair to interpret this as Jesus not saying forgive up to 490 times, but that your forgiveness should take on no limit because God has no limit to forgiving you. Holding onto what you have spoiled the gift.

More intriguing, we see Jesus on the cross, "Forgive them, they know not what they do". Forgiving and asking the Father to forgive his murderers and mockers. (Luke 23:24 NASB2020)

In Colossian 3:13 – the apostle Paul encourages "bearing with one another and forgiving each other, whoever has a complaint against anyone, just as the Lord forgave you, so also should you." (NASB2020)

Ephesians 4:32 – "Be kind to one another, tender-hearted, forgiving each other, just as God in Christ also has forgiven you."(NASB2020)

And there are numerous other accounts in the scriptures that admonish the effort to forgive one another. But what needs to be understood here is why this is necessary. It has been sort of perplexing to me why the purpose of forgiveness has not been explained. All I can do is trust that He wants us to rely on our instinct which suggests we know this to be a good and healthy endeavor. Yet here I am compelled to sort this out for us because in my working with people, I have all too often seen forgiveness handled with an ineffective we approach. Meaning, approaching forgiveness without really resolving the true issue at hand. As indicated earlier, forgiveness has mostly to do with anger.

I want to point to a very old sermon by Joseph Butler in 1726. Butler's sermons of 1726 on forgiveness might provide the finest Christian explanations of this topic. Many modern critics refer to him as they approach this concept from a Christian perspective. Thus, it is important to consult Butler's sermons before we explore the recent critical evaluations of forgiveness from a Christian perspective.

In sermons VIII and XI, Butler discusses anger in relation to forgiveness. He starts with distinguishing two forms of anger: "Butler suggests that the term 'indignation' refers to that anger raised in us by a wrong to another, while 'resentment' refers to that emotion raised by a wrong to ourselves." Then, he wonders how "a loving and good God" could implant anger in humankind? In an attempt to answer this question, Butler claims that both types of anger are natural reactions to an offense and are designed to protect us from harming others (Newberry 235).

At the same time, Butler urges people to control their anger and not allow it to develop into actions because, according to Butler and Mathew (43-44), Christianity is about loving the other with all the possible meaning invested in the word "other".

"Ye have heard that it hath been said; Thou shalt love thy neighbor, and hate thine enemy. But I say unto you, love your enemies, bless them that curse you, do good to them that hate you, and pray for them which despitefully use you and persecute you." (Newberry 235)

Butler deduces that the command to forgive is directed at both resentment and indignation because he thinks that revenge always inflicts more pain and harm than it reduces anger. In Christianity as Butler explains, *revenge is an inexcusable action because it does not accomplish the purpose of resentment, which is to protect against injury or harm (Newberry 236).* Instead, Butler directs people to love their offenders and enemies, which he thinks is not possible if we are angry with them since "the only thing that stands between us and love of all of our neighbors, even those who have harmed us, is the excess and abuse of resentment" (Newberry 237). Therefore, he invites people to forgive each other.

The meaning of forgiveness is found in "Love your enemy"

I love Butler's use of Jesus' teaching on "love your enemy". I would add, however, that a way of reducing anger toward someone is to intentionally, consciously show love. And over time the anger will decrease in its weight. There is a psychological lesson Jesus presents in the "love your enemy" statement that is worth paying attention to. Again, we need to ask, "Why is he saying this?" If there is one thing I want you to grab from this chapter it's this right here! And because it is essential, I will quote the text again.

> Matthew 5:43: *"You have heard that it was said, "You shall love our neighbor and hate your enemy.; But I say to you, love your enemies and pray for those who persecute you."*

So why? Try to remember a time when you were very angry at someone; or when someone who had deeply offended you. Maybe you have an actual 'enemy'. They have wronged you and your family. And there you are sitting with your anger. What does that anger feel like? How does it sit with you? How easy has it been to share the story with another so you can taste that bittersweet indignation? How much of you actually has taken pleasure in the power of that anger toward that other? Yet, at the same time, is there something disturbing about how much that person has become a powerful presence in your life and home?

Anger grows to this overwhelming resentment. And if we ignore the 2 paths of resentment, 'get over it and move on; or figure out how to solve the damn problem and be responsible', then we go the third and tragic route which is the big deal here. When we grow the anger in us, we start to become the very thing that hurt us.

You see, Jesus was trying to teach us here that by not loving our enemy, the anger and fear grows and in time your enemy wins; and you are now vulnerable to become just like the thing you hate, your enemy. Without going into great detail here, it is not a hard mystery to solve in how victims become perpetrators if they don't treat their wounds carefully. Note here, Jesus does not say to "love your enemies" from a place of emotion, but rather it is a decision.

Simply, showing *acts* of love and kindness toward someone you hate starts to lessen the weight of anger and something else grows. Show love long enough and love grows in one's heart. This might be exemplified in the malevolence of Hitler. His disdain for the Jewish race grew to a heightened level of gross evil because he fed the hate with more vile hatred, allowing for more insidious acts toward the Jews.

Hatred grows into more hatred if not addressed appropriately. Love your enemies, and that would naturally involve the gift of forgiveness. And to help I want to offer a way in which you can try to approach this. See, Jesus and his pastors have it right. Forgiving is essential for the soul of another, it is just not a good thing to do.

In conclusion, God is pointing toward forgiveness in order that we might be restoring the battle for the condition of all our souls. Forgiveness heals the soul of the one who is hurt/angered, and it heals the soul of the one who offered the hurt which is dying of guilt and shame.

Impact of Forgiveness and Unforgiveness on Mental Health

Forgiveness has a tremendous impact on one's mental and physical health. Studies have found that the act of forgiveness can reap huge rewards for your health, lowering the risk of heart attack; improving cholesterol levels and sleep; and reducing pain, blood pressure, and levels of anxiety, depression, and stress. And research points to an increase in the forgiveness-health connection as you age. When one decides to forgive, it is a genuine decision to no longer hold something against another person. When the resentment, or anger is forgiven by the one who has been hurt, then that person decides to 'let go' of that 'state'/ sentiment, etc. In doing so, a sense of freedom and even self-control starts to take place; almost immediately. When that occurs, when freedom is realized, it can allow one to have a sense of peace; and contentment; no longer bound by the perceived power of another's actions. This can help improve one's overall mental health.

The effect of not forgiving another person has great potential to hold onto negative feelings and ideas that tend to grow and fraction off inside one's own soul. It can even filter one's perspective/outlook creating a negative or even toxic emotional landscape inside. Harboring negative emotions/unforgiveness can affect our mood. It becomes added stress to carry; added stress affects the immune system often promoting poor health. Unforgiveness may also inhibit relationships in general. Holding onto that wound creates a specific belief and mistrust about people and gets in the way of forming trusting and nurturing relationships; simply due to harboring past hurts, resentments etc.

In general terms, forgiveness promotes a sense of emotional and mental freedom. Un-forgiveness can foster/promote a negative emotional inner world resulting in difficult relationships and even compromised health. Ultimately, what we hold onto, we potentially become. I want you to sit with that idea, and reflect.

List of symptoms of Un-forgiveness

- Carrying over anger and bitterness into all other current and future relationships.
- Difficulty being able to be in the moment; wrapped up in the past or "what if."
- Becoming more depressed and anxious.
- Feeling at odds with your spiritual beliefs.
- Compromised health/immune system.
- Difficulty making the kind of close relationships you desire.
- PTED-Post Traumatic Embitterment Disorder.

Mental Health Benefits of Forgiveness

- Less anxiety and depression.
- Improved relationship functioning.
- Improved self-esteem.
- Feeling less bound by the past or a victim to life.
- Feeling more in control of your being and not bound by someone else's actions.
- Empowerment to come from a position of strength to restore another who has acted in a wrong manner. It also empowers the ones who are offended; they are unburdened with the offense of their doing; and can also live more freely.

Mental and Physical Health Impacts of Un-forgiveness

- Effects of anger and resentment on the brain create toxic imprints. Splashes of cortisol in the brain can create damaging effects.
- Studies show that repressed anger can be harmful to our bodies and our minds. Not everyone knows how to manage their anger or how to express it. Holding back anger can

lead to mental illnesses including depression. One way of looking at depression is as anger turns inward. An emotion such as anger will not go away if ignored. It will only get stronger and can cause severe problems. Studies indicate that angry and aggressive behavior that goes unchecked can eventually cause changes to the brain that will decrease the production of serotonin and increase the chances of angry and aggressive behavior (Society for Neuroscience, 2007).

- Forgiveness may contribute to SWB (Social Well-Being). Despite a dearth of studies, existing research suggests reasons to expect a relationship between forgiveness and SWB. For instance, psychological well-being (i.e., a specific operationalization of well-being including personal autonomy, environmental mastery, personal relationships with others, personal life, personal growth, and self-acceptance) is a protective factor for the health of elderly adults. In a study by Lawler-Row, K. A., & Piferi, R. L. (2006). with elderly adults, those who endorsed a more forgiving disposition scored higher on the six dimensions of psychological well-being than those who did not endorse a forgiving disposition.

Effects of Anger and resentment toward health

For instance, individuals with anorexia, bulimia, and other eating disorders not otherwise specified (EDNOS) have reported significantly lower levels of self-forgiveness, as compared to controls (Watson, Lydecker, Jobe, Enright, Gartner). Self-forgiveness intervention programs increased self-forgiveness and reduced their feelings of shame and guilt related to drinking behavior. Thus, self-forgiveness appears to reduce guilt and shame emotions and destructive behaviors.

Forgiveness – The Exhale

How might I forgive?

When talking about forgiveness, I think its of great importance to take on a serious look at the forgiveness of self. This, I must say, shows up in the office as much or more often than forgiving others. The sticky and weighty presence of un-forgiveness toward ourselves is a real dilemma. We have mechanisms of stuffing our feelings of hurt. We perform psychological acrobatics that allow us to dismiss people who wrong us. People outside of us are not our responsibility. However, when it comes to ourselves and the sins we commit to others, it creates the soul cancer of shame.

We commit some kind of social, interpersonal relationship emotional/behavioral crime and instantly the feelings of guilt hit is. Guilt, is the negative horrific emotion we feel about ourselves due to something bad we committed. And if we don't have ways of resolving guilt, guilt sits around in the mind/heart of us and it grows. It grows into something more. Guilt expands itself into a self-image, self-belief of who we now think we are, a bad person that now manifests itself as shame.

Shame has always seemed like a deep-seated belief-feeling. It suggests that because of something bad we have done; we are a bad person. It is a messy emotion and, when not resolved, it only promotes a viscous cycle of more self-defeating behaviors. So, what is the way out of this emotional hell?

I often consider the phrase by Pastor Jim Griffin in regards to self-forgiveness. "You can't give what you don't have." I had to ponder that for a while. How can we forgive ourselves or anyone else if we don't seem to possess it in some capacity? An interesting concept. This sort of starts me to ponder how the forgiveness of something bigger than I, God, Jesus, fills me in some way. His eternal forgiveness is an understanding, a place to access, and a behavior I get to model.

When I need to forgive others, I have a pool of forgiveness I can access. When I fall, I can go to God as a reminder of eternal forgiveness. Second, when I fall and offend another, realizing the yearning for their forgiveness is so vital to my recovery. Receiving forgiveness is transforming. The experience delivers so much release, and breath! RUACH. It is like chains around your soul get clipped by big chain breakers. The chains of guilt and shame loudly hit the ground, and you automatically feel like you want to be a better person.

Gratitude overwhelms us when forgiveness is extended. The soul just got a blast of oxygen. I wanted to put together a way of stepping through how we may go about forgiving ourselves and others.

Toward Yourself – some things you can say to yourself

1. I agree that I am not shrunk down to my behaviors. Who does God see/proclaim me to be?
2. I agree I am not the be-all and end all, and that I am trying to learn, and God became my sin by dying on the Cross.
3. I agree that if I don't accept the fact I was, at some point, going to fall then I have lived in a false sense of identity for quite a long time.
4. My mistake was there for me to learn what UP really means. I got to learn what those sins were trying to teach me. Letting our sins finally teach us without condemning ourselves. We sit at the foot of the cross, in blood-stained dirt, basking in His forgiveness so that we can learn, forgive, and get up and walk with a heart full of forgiveness.

Forgiving others (and may apply to self as well)

1. Assess what just happened and consider the idea of forgiving.

2. Discern: Is anger more important than another kind of power?
3. Investigate why I think this happened. Why might they have done this? Ask.
4. In consideration of their "why," can come to an understanding of why they did what they did bring up some compassion? While trying not to confuse rationale as condoning behavior.
5. With compassion comes reasoning; with reasoning comes understanding; with understanding now brings up the possibility to forgive.
6. In considering forgiveness, we weigh the need to keep and hold onto anger or let it go and embrace grace, mercy, and forgiveness.
7. Whether or not they ask for your forgiveness and/or don't take responsibility for their actions, you still have the choice here to forgive or not.
8. Take back the power by giving them forgiveness to restore them and make them better as a person.
9. You release your soul from the anger and resentment.
10. Forgive. You can say these things:
"I can forgive you because you need it and so do I."
"I accept your plea and apology; I can forgive you."
"I can forgive you and do forgive you, but I may need time to figure out how we continue on."

Forgiveness offers freedom for both parties involved. The one who is offended upon can be free of anger, resentment, etc. And the one forgiven is free from condemnation, guilt, and sorrow. So, I harken back to the story of Alisha. It might be fair to conceptualize we all may find ourselves in the elevator with the enemy. Finding ourselves close to becoming the murderer toward the murderer and justified for it. But becoming the murderer is the real defeat. We find ourselves in these dire stories where our choices can determine whether we become the hero or we become the villain. And what determines our breath in life is how we handle this choice of forgiveness or no forgiveness. What we hold onto we potentially become. So when faced with that moment, you are in the elevator with the enemy, walk. Walk up to the enemy and love it, pardon it, and embrace it. When loving the enemy, you find the hatred leaving. And loving the enemy is your victory.

In conclusion, I started with the traveling metaphor where we are limited in what we can take with us for our travels. Our suitcase can only hold so much luggage. As is with our hearts, it is of wise discernment we are careful what we 'hold on to'. Love, resentment, gratitude, hate, anger, hope, kindness etc. With all compassion and understanding, I know it is hard to let go of hurt and anger. Some of the tragedies that afflicted us create profound wounds. Wounds take on a sacredness as well, that I won't get into here. In some rare instances, I have seen wounds that were left unattended to because un-forgiveness had a functioning role. These wounds give us the anger we need to survive, and sort of take on this sacred meaning.

But for all other intents and purposes, we are challenged to figure out the letting go so the heart suitcase serves us well. We get to decide what we travel with our suitcases. Be wise in what is worth traveling with. Further, we can have breath for ourselves and give breath to others. We have this responsibility, as I see it, to make ourselves better and also call others into being better human beings and God's image bearers. And this is possible by being aware, along the road, of how we find a breath of forgiveness for us and one another.

If I were to take that U2 album title and turn it into a question, "What can be the one thing that you can't leave behind?" How would you answer it? I answer it this way: *Love and forgiveness are all that I cannot leave behind.*

KEITH HUGHES, M.A.

Love is not an easy thing
The only baggage you can bring
Is all that you can't leave behind
    —U2 "Walk On"

RARELY ARE THINGS AS THEY SEEM

The Breath of New Perspective – Reframing Our Life

*"But everything you see's not the way it seems—
Tears can sing and joy can shed a tear"*
—B. Cockburn (Hills of Morning, 1979)

KEITH HUGHES, M.A.

Opening Prayer

Lord, high and holy, meek and lowly. You have brought me to the valley of vision, where I live in the depths but see you in the heights; hemmed in by mountains of sin I behold your glory. Let me learn by paradox that the way down is the way up, that to be low is to be high, that the broken heart is the healed heart, that the contrite spirit is the rejoicing spirit, that the repenting soul is the victorious soul, that to have nothing is to possess all, that to bear the cross is to wear the crown, that to give is to receive, that the valley is the place of vision. Lord, in the daytime stars can be seen from the deepest wells, and the deeper the wells the brighter your stars shine; let me find your light in my darkness, your life in my death, your joy in my sorrow, your grace in my sin, your riches in my poverty, your glory in my valley.

Author Unknown[1]

A COMMON THEORY and saying is, "perception is reality. Or 85% of life is perception." But what we need to understand here is, yes, we all have our own 'perception' of ourselves and situations. But the second half of better understanding or even adjusting our perceptions if finding *perspective*. Our perception of things, if we are honest, may not be accurate, true, real or productive. At times we are in dire need of finding a perspective of our situation or ourselves that can be more productive. To get out of ourselves, and look outside ourselves. To find another point of view. What happens if we do not take the time to consider another point of view? A majority of my clinical work consists of working with people needing to find another perspective on their situation, i.e. personal suffering, relationships etc. By not discovering a new view of their situation their oxygen, soul oxygen, becomes grossly depleted. It is incredibly exhausting to be locked into looking at

---

[1] Arthur Bennett, ed., *The Valley of Vision: A Collection of Puritan Prayers and Devotions* (Edinburgh: Banner of Truth Trust, 1975).

something in one way, sucking the air out of your life. Most of our problems deserve, even demand, a new look at them, so we can live with our dilemmas better. Or we can overcome the tragedy because we have a new vision of it. Take relationships for example. If all we did was approach them from our own point of view, would we ever be able to resolve conflict or learn about the other person? No! What if we never found a new way to look at life? We would never grow!

There are numerous ways to look at most things in our life! If we don't, life will remain empty and tragic. If our beliefs never change then we live out the same patterns and behaviors only producing the same outcomes. So if we are invested in changing our lives, in how we act, feel, think and believe, then we need to have a new perspective on how we and what we believe. If we don't take the time to find alternative perspectives in a moment, a person, or a conversation, then much of life will crush us and we'll miss out on better ways to construct meaning out of our circumstances.

The ability to find new perspectives in life's dilemmas directly correlates with our ability to contend with pain. Developing the skill of reframing is the pathway to creating meaning through all things malevolent. Evil, self-inflicted wounds, and the world in which we live can deliver many circumstances full of pain and discomfort. As a result, we are left to figure out how to cope. The malevolence of life is unavoidable. How we cope determines our quality of life. Coping with sin, evil, and pain requires finding new ways to look at our situations. By finding ways to reframe our problems and pain, we gain breath and insight into our existence. Further, we are better able to manage our lives and ultimately thrive.

Reframing isn't just applicable for painful dilemmas, but also for high-water mark moments. Some of us can relate to times in which things in life are fantastic, yet we're mysteriously overrun by anxiety, uncertainty, or even sadness. Contradictory feelings require sorting, and reframing can help us contend with complex and contradictory feelings and thoughts.

When good things happen, sometimes the heart has difficulty catching up. Our heart doesn't always run at the speed life runs. In contrast, sometimes the opposite may be true—life may not keep pace with our heart and its desires. The brain can process blessings as optical illusions. This results in cognitive dissonance. Beliefs, expectations, history, and the current situation are all trying to align together. This causes mixed, confused emotions toward what appears to be a fortunate event.

Inhale

Our fascination with magic goes back thousands of years. We have always had a yearning to see beyond the natural or transcend beyond the here and now. I'll admit, I get intrigued by every Criss Angel trick. The incredible talent of manipulating perception and making something fake appear real is remarkable to me. The allure of "magic" or manipulation of reality seems to be deeply embedded in us. This might be related to our desire to be connected to something bigger than ourselves.

The definition of spirituality may simply be explained as when we have the sense/experience/understanding that we are connected to something bigger. I think we can admit we desire to try to manipulate or change how we see the world. Further, we desire to have the ability to look upon our lives and suffering in new way so we can cope with it. Many magicians confess that all magic is just the craft of presenting the illusion in a way that makes it seem real.

For certain, life is tragic, and what we don't want to do is indulge tragedy and live in hell. Suffering without meaning is hell—try denying that. Suffering presents the need to learn this magnificent ability we have, which is to reframe life when tragedy occurs or when things are perplexing and painful. One of the biggest obstacles I've observed in clients is their inability to contend with their pain while gaining perspective. They are often unable to create a working perspective on the situation so that they can begin to engage with the problem and calm down from the initial upheaval, fear, anxiety, or hopelessness.

Too often our emotions tend to be the initial interpreter of the situation. And as a result, we tend to see the situation only from the lens of our emotions. However, what we need to understand is that what we see *is not* exactly what is happening. My clinical mantra is "*Rarely are things as they seem.*" Hold onto that. Don't forget it. It is true. Simple, yes, but it's a rock-solid truth. What you see from others or in circumstances is most likely a cover-up. There is always more than what meets the eye. That phrase comes from the great Dr. Arlene Martinez Meads, my first supervisor. There is always more to a person, a title, a situation, than what we see on the surface or at first glance. There is always something more going on below the surface, and there are clues about what's going on that we often fail to notice.

According to cognitive neuroscientists, we are conscious of only about 5 percent of our cognitive activity, so most of our decisions, actions, emotions, and behavior depend on the 95 percent of brain activity that goes beyond our conscious awareness. (Mysteries of the mind Your unconscious is making your everyday decisions By Marianne Szegedy-Maszak). *Two of the essential principles for living sensibly in this world are: knowing how to reframe your past and present circumstances and knowing that more is happening below the surface.*

Reframing (finding new perspective) is so important that I had to start this book by introducing this skill. Looking at something only one way is what I call a cripple vision. All circumstances, people, ideas, concepts, and beliefs have numerous ways one can look at them. This is a critical skill because it provides us with the ability to make more sense of what is happening to us and to do so in a way that makes life more meaningful. Being able to reframe our lives brings breath to us. And helping others see things in a new way brings breath to them. Not being able to find a new perspective on tragic, difficult, painful, and/or complex situations can take the breath right out of us and choke us with pain.

I want to give an example of reframing. Let's start with a generalized example of a past tragedy.

Painful event occurs
Painful event try to teach us something about ourselves and the world:
 I am not valued. The world is not predictable or safe. The world is painful. I am weak and powerless. These are many of the things learned from a tragic event. Any of the barriers we thought existed between us and evil have been taken away or exposed as untrue. And now it has hit us, and we are left with pain.

Painful event is stored in the memory system of the brain:
 Traumatic events ignite an explosion of hormones (cortisol, adrenaline, and more) throughout the brain creating new neurological pathways. These pathways create highways in the brain when any other event occurs that might trigger this memory and cause hormones to run through them again. Memories are stored, and when something comes along to trigger a memory, there is a physical response in the body that triggers an emotional response. The brain and body never forget.
 The painful event creates a bleak feeling and takes on a negative meaning. Initially, anything painful takes on some sort of negative meaning—whether it reinforces hopelessness, shame, guilt, anger, lack of security, or disappointment.

Painful event is assessed:
 We assess the event. We ask questions such as: Why? How? What really happened? Then we assess the losses and impact. How deep of an impact is this? How might I get back up? What are ways I have compensated for my losses and developed new ways of living? What new understandings have I acquired from the event? What are the facts versus only perceptions? What can I or can't I do? How has it impacted how I see myself and others?

Painful event is observed creates certain skills in us:
 The painful event teaches pain tolerance. Our capacity for empathy is increased, which increases our ability to understand and connect with others. Pain increases the capacity for compassion

which in turn teaches us how to care for others more effectively. Pain gives us knowledge about the nature of evil. And why would I mention that? Evil is not something you want to be naïve about. It is hard to respect something if you know nothing about it.

We learn the skill of conversion—that is, turning what was meant for bad into good. Relative to the often-quoted words from the apostle Paul, "God works all things (causes all things) to work together for the good to those who love God, to those called according to His purpose," (Romans 8:28 NASB 2020).

By learning how life can be tragic and fragile, there is a paradoxical response that sometimes occurs where we gain a sense of gratitude. We offer that gratitude back to the world through service to others. Contending with painful events also teaches what is true and false about the world. We live only with head knowledge about certain things, but real tragedy brings to the surface how things in life work. We learn that we can heal. And that is a big event. To know you heal seems to cause a certain strength to grow inside of us.

We learn that we can endure more than we thought. Again, to quote the Apostle Paul, "Celebrate in your suffering, know that tribulations bring about perseverance; and perseverance proven character; and proven character brings hope." (Romans 5:3-5NASb 2020) The apostle shows a great progression here how contending with suffering works.

First, celebrate or "rejoice" in your suffering. That seems to be a counter-intuitive idea when the pain and suffering of tribulations occur. Rejoicing, and celebrating is a psychological combatant to pain. It causes us to release positive brain chemicals in our body to combat sadness and grief. Also, it helps us seek some acceptance and responsibility for our situation which is important in recovering. And like he states, rejoicing keeps us going in the fight, helping us persevere. We cannot persevere if we are strapped down by despair and anguish. As we persevere, internal muscles and fortitude grow inside of us, character. To persevere through anything difficult gives great odds to growing internal strength and resolve in life. Once we have become aware of the strength building inside us then that produces hope. We have oxygen in us that provides hope that says, "I can make it. Regardless of the outcome, I will be well".

The skills we learn can be utilized productively and help us find purpose:
Our new skills help us serve others. They help us become great teachers with credibility and insight. They help us become healers for others who are afflicted. They help us become advocates for those still suffering. Many people discover their lifelong occupations out of their own recovery, whether that be substance abuse, grief, physical injuries, trauma, etc. Additionally, through learnings from our recovery, we can help others grow from their own pain and suffering. Which brings us to the next lesson.

The lessons we learn become our wisdom and—paradoxically—our gifting:
Wisdom can be birthed from pain and suffering. Wisdom makes us more discerning for ourselves and others. Suffering becomes a gift because it fills the mind with understanding and the heart with compassion and compels us to be better—if we decide to allow our pain to have meaning in the first place. Pain and suffering without meaning is hell. Take for example my father-in-law Joe Martinez. He lived a life far from compassion and mercy, but after cancer entered his life, he found a new heart of compassion and mercy for the poor and wanted to serve them. Joe was grateful for every day he got to breathe and live around his family. "I thank God for cancer, it helped me be a better person."

Painful event now holds new meaning as sacred event:
These skills aren't just psychological—they're also spiritual. As mentioned earlier, Paul the Apostle writes to the Romans that "all things work together for the good" (Romans 8:28). What was chaotic, dark, and evil, God can reframe and transform into something meaningful and good. But it takes a conscious effort on our end to engage this psychological/spiritual principle. All of life is waiting to be understood in more meaningful and redemptive ways.

For many of us, words like "redemption" and "transformation" are just nice religious words we read, sing about, and talk about. We're not aware of what they actually look like or how to experience them.

We are wired to understand, experience, and participate in redemption and transformation. For instance, all of us have some kind of weakness or vulnerability. We might even want to identify it as a "thorn" in the flesh. Much like we see in 2 Corinthians 12:7-10 where Paul says, "I was given a thorn in my flesh, a messenger of Satan, to torment me. Three times I pleaded with the Lord to take it away from me. But he said to me, 'My grace is sufficient for you, for my power is made perfect in weakness'… I delight in weakness, for when I am weak, then I am strong."

These are powerful and perplexing words from Paul. We take from this the understanding that our flesh may be imprinted by an affliction (e.g., addiction, mental health disorders, desire disorders, and other vulnerabilities) but it is in our weakness that we discover our greatest spiritual potential. We discover the depth of the Holy Spirit's potential in our life. This specific teaching by the apostle Paul exemplifies what I am saying. If we can reframe our weakness as place to access strength, then we have a fighting chance of contextualizing our weakness. One could view Paul's idea here as when we are vulnerable (weakness), we open ourselves to a new kind of power. Vulnerability is an act of power, and courage.

Vulnerability can put us into a position of reliance, relying on God, not of our own strength. Vulnerability, a posture of humility which is a quiet and graceful strength. There is a powerful song, by John Denver, lyrics of Joe Henry, called "The Flower that Shattered the Stone." What a concept, the tender, soft flower overpowers the stone. This lends to this concept of reframing weak and soft.. Kindness turns away wrath. Softness can disarm fear and defensiveness. Love can overcome hatred. Tenderness can break down the hardness of the heart. All that to say we have the power to change how we view things so that new meaning, deeper meaning, and true strength can be birthed in our lives.

The magic we can practice is staying in the moment. And when we stay in the moment, we can allow ourselves to investigate what we are noticing. Then we think about other ways to view our situation. Maybe we can imagine new ways to look at ourselves.

Reframing is a brain exercise. When we read in the scriptures the instruction and possibility of "renewing of our minds" (Romans 12:2NASB2020) and "to be made new in the attitude of your minds" (Ephesians 4:23 NASB2020), we understand that God is telling us that we can change the way we think about anything. This confirms free will. If you believe in free will—the freedom to choose—then we are admitting we can change how we think. Choosing a thought is a way to start reframing our view of ourselves and the world. There is an old saying that states, "How a man thinks, so is he."

What lives in our mind, such as our perspectives, beliefs, memories, and ideas, all have elasticity. Unfortunately, we usually don't believe this is the case. We tend to perceive things in our mind as set and static. But this simply is not true. We can view anything in a different way—even the facts about what happened in a certain memory, like the ending of a past relationship that broke your heart, the job you lost because of poor performance, our dumb mistakes, or the quick moment you did a bad or upsetting thing to someone.

For instance, that one terrible thing you did… what was the stage it happened on? What were you feeling? What was your thought at the time? Did you think the other person wouldn't see it so negatively? Did you think that it was a small, playful gesture? Do you wish you could take it back? You can take it back. And you can imagine how you might have done things differently. If given the time to repair, would you? Does the event show something about you that can get better? The worst-case scenario is most likely not going to happen. So, you can move on.

You can learn that you need saving just like everyone else—and that's a good thing. Embrace humility, not humiliation. You can look at what you have done, you can see how it happened, you can see how you made that choice, you can now see what it is you need more of in your life but through different means, and you can assure yourself that you're safe and that you will live better now because of it. It's ok. That bad moment exposes a piece of your brokenness. And that brokenness needs and wants to be healed. You are not in trouble. Move forward with grace. Reframing is a gift and a spiritual act of magic from God. As the Apostle Paul says, "all things work together for the good" (Romans 8:28).

The Gift of Metaphor

Life can seem large sometimes. So large that we can't make sense of it. It's a minute-by-minute, hour-by-hour, day-by-day deluge of so much content that it's hard to have any perspective on what is happening to us. Reflection is an essential skill because it helps us interpret and process events and feelings. Without reflection, life stays large, chaotic, and overwhelming. Reflection allows us to find metaphors that help us frame our lives. Using metaphors to interpret our lives is one of the most common skills I use and encourage others to apply to their life. It is essential. *Giving language, images, and sounds to our feelings* and experiences is a way we can relate to them. Even if the metaphor is wild or strange, it still gives us a picture that helps us cope with our situation. It is why art is a critical ingredient in life. Art helps us access metaphors to express, interpret, and understand life in a myriad of ways. This is why I am an avid lover of music, theatre, dance, cinema, stories, and sports.

For Example

1. Throughout my life, or on any given day/week, I may find myself overwhelmed, and perplexed, as life becomes too big or stressful. One of my favorite metaphors comes from the game of tennis. I played in my sophomore year in high school and also played a lot in my young adult years. Visualizing the act of hitting the tennis ball back and forth is a sort of meditation. Many concepts in the game

of tennis apply to understanding some of life's situations. For instance, sometimes, like in tennis, you need to just play conservatively, not taking risks, just *keeping the ball in play* and keeping yourself *"in the game"*. Nothing more. Nothing less. By taking this approach, you are maintaining and building upon momentum. And good momentum builds confidence. No need to swing big for the crushing winner! Especially if you are struggling in the match and not playing well, if you just keep the ball in play, you will avoid overextending yourself and causing an unforced error. Back and forth, over and over again… Keep control and a conservative pace. Your opportunity to hit a successful winner *will* present itself. Be patient. Access your stamina. When your opportunity to be aggressive appears, then go for that smashing winner!

I find life doesn't always ask me to go for the winner, but to just be calm and consistent, and *keep it in play*. I may not be in a great motivated space or may be feeling low or stressed, so I just approach my days by, "keeping the ball in play", don't try too hard, do what are the basics, stay in the game. We often just have to show up and keep the ball in play. You don't have to hit a winner every time. In sports we call this "pressing"—that is, when you try too hard or try to do too much.

So, at any point in my day—at the office, in the car, lying down at night—I think about some of the epic tennis matches between the greats: Agassi vs Sampras, Connors vs McEnroe, Nadal vs Federer. They were geniuses in smartly keeping the ball in play. By keeping the ball in play helps us wait for that moment to hit the winner. Being patient can change the momentum of a match and ultimately assist in your comeback. I can picture my current situation and imagine myself showing up and keeping myself in the moment. At some point, I will take my shot. This tennis metaphor has helped me monitor my stress and has given me permission to admire the routine of work and life.

2. Life can feel like losing or being behind in the score. This calls for a good metaphor. The big comeback. At some point in our lives, we all have been there, right? You're losing at work, losing in your relationship, you're at your lowest, most desperate moment emotionally, financially, mentally, physically… Now what do you do? We look up at life's scoreboard and shake our head, saying "I don't know how I can get through this or how I can win. I am so far behind." You're in that situation saying, "I just can't go on. I can't possibly see how this gets better or how I get through this." So what in next??

Wait for that moment. In these times/ seasons, we get to wait and watch for that *one moment* when something occurs that *shifts* the momentum. It can be anything. A small break. An advantageous opportunity. Sometimes those moments are small or big. But they do show up. Momentum changes. Fittingly, the tennis great, Andre Agassi, says in his self-revealing autobiography, "Open", "Life is about momentum. You work to keep or create *good* momentum because bad momentum is a bitch to stop."(Caponi, Paolo. 2014. "Andre Agassi, Open") When losing, or behind in the score in life, we look at it like a game. Whether it is tennis, football, or any other game when being behind, there sometimes comes a moment, sometimes small, that triggers something great. There is a break: a base hit, one forehand winner in tennis, one mistake by the opposition, one turnover, one spectacular catch and it ignites hope! One small ignition of hope can start the beginning of a flame, turning into a fire, turning into a forest fire. We know one spark can cause a forest fire. See a metaphor. In our own life wait for that spark, or create a spark and flame it.

As an example, I recall two epic moments in sports that helped me when I was in that situation. First, the 1991 U.S. Open. Jimmy Connors beat all the odds against him and came back multiple times at the age of 39. Down 0 sets to 4, he pushed the match past midnight, by keeping the ball in play, he just kept hitting the ball, one shot after another, and after many patient hits, he produced turning points, and sparks, that gave him hope. He gave it his absolute best effort, even when it seemed like he would lose. When most would have been psychologically defeated, he shifted momentum back to himself, and Connors just gave his guts to every shot and never quit. It's as if he was telling his opponent, the crowd, and the world, "You're gonna have to kill me to get me off this court. If you don't have the guts to kill me, you're going to watch me win." Perhaps that's something we can say to our adversity, "If you don't have the guts to beat me, you're going to watch me win'. And win he did. At the age of 39 he made it to the semi-finals that year. In the mind of most spectators and journalists, that tournament was won by Jimmy Connors because of the way he played. Coming from behind in 3 matches in a row. He was losing, and he waited, he found those moments, found and created sparks to ignite a forest fire of inspiration.

The second moment is John Elway's epic career-defining moment, referred to as "The Drive." On their own 2-yard line, mere minutes to go in the game, down 6 points, John Elway had nerves of steel amidst adversity. With just over 5 minutes left in the AFC Championship game, Elway led his Denver Broncos 98 yards down the field in 15 plays to tie the score, and they ended up winning in overtime. What a great picture of how to come back. Comebacks are great metaphors to use when we are down and behind in life. When we draw from metaphors such as the ones above, we can find hope and determination not to give up.

There are other metaphors you can use—mountain climbing, skiing, marathons, or any sport. Metaphors give us a way to interpret life. I like to use music for a metaphor. Some days are like heavy metal, some are like soft jazz, and some are like pop. We need metaphors for help in our relationships, our work, and when we work through tragedies. Metaphors are a way we reframe our lives, add meaning to our lives, and make our lives more manageable.

Distortions

Life is hard when we look at it through a distorted lens. The most common distorted lens is black-and-white or all-or-nothing thinking. You may be familiar with this. In this type of thinking, we take the approach that there is a right way and a wrong way. It's either THIS or THAT, it's either GREAT or HORRIBLE, there is ONE way or NO way. This prevents us from ever looking at life with any kind of creativity or flexibility. We put people and what they do in boxes. The obvious problem with this sort of thinking is it doesn't allow for any gray area. But we know life has a gray area.

Another common form of distorted thinking is jumping to conclusions. I have witnessed this in a variety of ways with various people, and it's usually a reactionary way to think. When something is presented to us, we jump to an imaginary end of how we fear it is going to turn out. And what usually occurs is we either become frustrated with the scenario, sabotage ourselves, or become humbled by the real outcome. When jumping to conclusions, we resort to filling in the missing information with negative assumptions.

And then there's the self-fulfilling prophecy way of thinking. If we can conclude what will happen before the story starts or finishes, we feel that life is somehow predictable and safe. I love one of Bono's stories. As he, Brian Eno, and Daniel Lanois were analyzing the structure of a song during one of their recording sessions for *The Unforgettable Fire*, Bono asks, "Have you ever heard of the story of Johnny Magori?" They respond, "No." And Bono said, "Shall I begin it? That's all that's in it." This is a rhyme that exemplifies finishing before starting.

How often do we do this in how we approach situations? This way of thinking is a way to not really allow life to happen in front of you. It is our way to duck away from life happening. The antidote to this is to stop telling a story in your head about how you think things will happen. Having a story in our head of how something is going to play out gives us a certain sense—though a false one—of how we think it's going to happen. It's as if we have some deep understanding of the universe affording us a way to know what will happen.

Now, these are just two kinds of distortions out of at least 15. But I wanted to illustrate for us an example of negative ways of framing life. Reframing is more about looking at ourselves and our situations in a way that brings productivity and meaning.

Belief

There is substantial power in belief. What we believe is foundational to what we think, and the rest dovetails from there. We all hold beliefs about everything in life, big and small—God, religion, sports, marriage, politics, education, morality, relationships, etc. Our beliefs are developed through many different aspects of life—our experiences, what we have been told, what we have observed, and what we have assumed.

Right now, I want to think about belief in terms of believing in something without seeing it. If we look closer into our life, there have been times when we didn't know whether something would come to pass. We had no reason to believe that whatever was before us would actually work. Yet we still embarked on it. We still marched down that road. We went ahead and acted on belief.

Why do I bring this up regarding reframing our lives? Well, to reframe our circumstances, we need belief to accept that there might be another way to see things. Not to do so would result in a pessimistic view of life or the secular view that believes "this is it." We need belief so that we can really believe that our thoughts can be restructured. Most of us exercise some kind of faith even if you consider yourself to be an atheist or non-believer. None of us know what is going to happen in the coming minutes, days, weeks, and years, yet we proceed in some form of belief. We all practice belief in something and someone at some point.

We need open-minded belief if we are to learn new perspectives on life. When we allow ourselves to consider there may be another way to perceive life, our life becomes more malleable, creative, dynamic, and even mystic. Whether we admit it or not, we have blindness. In one form or another, we cannot see things that are in front of us. We are unable to see life in its fullest, which is why we need one another to help us see. Also, it may be possible to stop ourselves, gaze at the moment, and say, "Although this is what I see, I wonder if there is another way to see it?" Sometimes when we say that we can "see" it is at that moment we are blind. Jesus eloquently points out to the Pharisees that when a man says he sees but ignores his sin, he is blind. But it's the man who knows he is blind—who knows he has sin—who is the one who actually sees. Jesus points out that we have our own internal blindness—arrogance, self-righteousness, stubbornness, pride, hatred, etc. All of these are ways we are blind, and blindness keeps us from believing.

Medical research supports that what we believe shapes our thinking and behaviors. Our beliefs affect our brain. Dr. Caroline Leaf, in her book *Switch On Your Brain*, says: "Research has recently been done by Dr. Gail Ironson, a leading mind-body medicine researcher and professor of psychology and psychiatry at the University of Miami. She found that a significant factor that made a difference in healing for those with HIV was their choice to believe in a benevolent and loving God, especially if they chose to have a personal relationship with a benevolent and loving God."

The four-year study simply evaluated how healing was based on the decrease of viral load—the amount of the AIDS virus in a sample of blood—and the increased concentration of Helper T-cells. The higher the concentration, the more the body is able to fight disease. She found that those who did not believe that God loved them lost helper T-cells three times faster. Their viral load also increased three times faster, and their stress levels were higher. Dr. Ironson summarizes that "If you believe God loves you, it's an enormously protective factor—even more protective than scoring low for depression or high for optimism. A view of a benevolent God is protective, *but* scoring high on the personalized statement 'God loves me' is even stronger." (Leaf, Switch On Your Brain pg 52). Believing that God loves us produces a chemical change that is healing. Imagine the state of our being if we didn't believe in God.

Another question to ask regarding beliefs is: What are your blind spots? Wherever in your life you hold tremendous ability and confidence can potentially be the places we become blind. Have you considered that you may be lacking sight, especially in areas of your greatest competence? There is danger in thinking you have reached "the promised land" in parts of your life. If you ever sense you may have "arrived" somewhere, it might be a red flag. We need to be able to continue learning and be able to see things from different perspectives. Admitting we may be blind to things right in front of us allows us to start seeing things in a new way. When we say to ourselves, "I don't know because I may be blind," the veil falls from our mind, images appear for the first time, and we start to see life with a brand-new lens.

Seeing things from a new perspective is very much like going from blindness to sight. I'll even go as far as to say that it is a spiritual act. It's God's way of demonstrating how He works. He has created the world in such a manner that all creation can be looked upon in various ways, and He did this to demonstrate His glory. Why wouldn't He want us to look at ourselves and our lives from various angles? Reframing gives us ways to get out of our traps of despair.

Happy people can develop the skill of recoding their negative experiences in a way that makes the experiences more meaningful. So when they "fail" at something, they reframe it by saying, "Well, yes, I didn't come in first, but I gave it all I had and did better. I also learned X, Y, Z, and I probably could have done this or that to win, which will help me next time." People who stay away from agony are able to change how they measure success. Comparing ourselves to others is a dangerous endeavor.

Reframing Success: The Silver Medalist Dilemma

Social scientists have pointed out a psychological phenomenon called "counterfactual thinking." The article, "Why Bronze Medalists Are Happier Than Silver Winners" by Jason G. Goldman

(Aug.9, 2012) discusses the roots of this phenomenon which can be traced back to early philosophers such as Aristotle and Plato. Counterfactual thinking is clearly illustrated by silver medal winners in the Olympics. What they found was very counter-intuitive. When we think of winning medals in the Olympics, we expect that everyone who wins a medal is happy. But researchers found a surprising twist. Almost everyone who trains for the Olympics trains to win the gold medal. When an athlete wins the gold, we see sheer joy on his or her face. Researchers studied the facial expressions of silver medalists when they received their medal. They had the medalists rank their joy on a scale of 1-10 (10 being the highest amount of joy, 1 being the lowest). What they found was interesting. Gold medalists ranked 9-10 on average, bronze medalists ranked 7, and silver medalists ranked 3-4. Goldman Aug. 9, 2012.

Silver medalists were the least happy of the medal winners. Why? Well, again, this is a lesson on perspective. How we see our circumstances makes a big difference in whether we experience joy or sorrow. So, what is it that determines whether we experience joy or sorrow? How the athletes defined success made all the difference. For instance, when the silver medalist comes in second, all the athlete sees is how he or she lost to the gold medalist. Additionally, when the silver medalist looks the other way, he or she perceives that he or she only beat one other person, the bronze medalist. As a result, the silver medalist destroys any joy he or she could have and winds up feeling defeated. The bronze medalist has more joy and satisfaction because he or she is happy to have finished in the top three—in other words, the bronze medalist is just happy he got a medal. Silver medal winners report more depression, more health issues, and they die younger. (Jason G. Goldman Aug.9, 2012)

Another illustration of reframing is the story of figure skating champion Michele Quan. She made it to the Olympic figure skating finals and was favorited to take the gold medal. But as history has it, she placed silver. Not only did she win a silver medal, but she was notably quite happy—smiling and waving upon accepting her medal. Afterwards, she said, "Sure, I wished I could have won the gold, but I am truly happy how things finished. I did better than what I actually anticipated." What made Michele Quan happy for winning the silver? She explained that she redefined her goals and what success looked like. She said that each and every day, she fell more in love with the process of training and of skating. She allowed herself to love the journey more than the destination. Sure, she wanted to win gold, but that wasn't the real goal. She wanted to skate her best and improve compared to how she competed before. None of that was being measured by a gold or silver medal. Michele loved the process and she competed against herself, not with her peers. As a result, the silver medal was… just the silver medal. And that allowed her to be happy for the winners and for herself.

Michele rearranged her perspective so that she could live with more joy. As I often emphasize when working with clients, the perceived "arrivals" we shoot for in life can be deceptive and make us bitter. Michele Quan teaches us that life is not so much about the destination but about the journey. It's about the person we are becoming. As Jesus said 2000 years ago, "What does a man profit if he gains the whole world, but loses his soul?"

How we currently look at ourselves, our circumstances, and our pursuits in life that may need reframing. Reframing is a gift that helps us change the way we see things so that we don't fall into traps of unnecessary pain. It also helps us find more meaning in life. Richard Rohr, in his book *The Universal Christ*, talks about how we sometimes *see things in front of us but don't recognize them*. What this suggests is that we often come upon things in life and we simply see them for what they immediately represent. If we aren't careful, we miss recognizing the deeper essence or meaning of things. For instance, take the story of Jesus on the road to Emmaus. Two followers of Jesus were walking down the road and were joined by the resurrected Jesus. They walked and talked with Jesus, but they didn't recognize that he was Jesus. You could say they saw him but didn't recognize him. It was when they sat and ate with him that they finally recognized him. If we're not mindful, we'll go through life just seeing what's in front of us instead of recognizing what we need to "see" or experience.

4 Breaths

Exhale

2 Corinthians 12:7-12

Another principle of reframing can be seen in the story of the apostle Paul regarding his "thorn in the flesh." This story is founded on the paradox "When I am weak, then I am strong." This is a challenging paradox. How are the disadvantages acting as advantages? How do we leverage weakness as a starting point of strength? These are questions I hope to answer in the "exhale" portion of this chapter.

We all have weaknesses, whether they be addictions, mental health conditions, disordered desires, physical or mental disabilities, vulnerabilities in our character or personality, etc. No matter how much we try to correct, manage, diminish, erase, or rehabilitate our weaknesses, their fingerprints are all over our lives. This is clearly and profoundly exemplified by the apostle Paul when he writes about pleading for God to remove the thorn in his flesh. There has been much speculation and debate among theologians and pastors about His "weakness" for centuries. The speculations range from Paul having a speech impediment, nightmares about murders he ordered, character flaw, demonic torment, poor eyesight, or an actual pain in his side. We can only speculate, but nonetheless it truly was a painful affliction.

What is intriguing is God's answer to Paul. Christ denies Paul's plea to remove the thorn three times! Christ says to Paul, "My grace is sufficient for you, for my power is perfected in weakness" (2 Corinthians 12:9). God leaves the thorn with Paul to keep him humble. This illustrates that God's way is counter-intuitive to man's way of thinking. God identifies that power comes from weakness, contrary to the human belief that power is found in strength. Instead, Paul learned that weakness is the pathway to seeing and experiencing the power of God. He is taught that weakness brings humility and reliance on God (instead of relying on one's own strength). Put simply, Paul's weakness brings him another kind of strength—the strength that comes from dependence on God, having faith, and exhibiting humility. *This suggests that our greatest spiritual potential is found in the depth of our weaknesses. A weakness calling us into our biggest strength, reliance on God, Spirit.* If Paul were to have his thorn removed, he becomes susceptible to boasting about himself and not relying on God.

My desire is that we will find breath by learning that strength is perfected in weakness. More specifically, I hope that we learn ways to live with our disadvantages and acknowledge the strength they produce. This will prevent us from falling into all-or-nothing thinking, which is a way of approaching life that fails to give us the life we want. It's an approach that says, "Well, it's either right or wrong, it's got to be this way or that way, I'm all in or all out, go big or go home." I am not saying there is no "right or wrong" or no moral code to follow. In other words, when we run into conflicts, our own behaviors, our limitations, or our contradictions, instead of immediately casting judgment on them, we should see the deeper meaning and what they can teach us. We need to learn how to accept and work within the truth about ourselves, including the weaknesses and contradictions that naturally present themselves. Our weaknesses and contradictions are gifts or blessings to help us live out a more spiritual understanding of self, God, and others in order to avoid unnecessary frustration and despair. Our disadvantages need to be investigated because they might present an accurate perception about our life.

Examples of Disadvantages vs Advantages

The ancient story of David and Goliath is an example of reframing advantages and disadvantages. We find David, described as a young shepherd, facing a battle with the Philistine giant, Goliath. The Israelite army was challenged by the Philistine army, and the Philistines demanded that the Israelites bring forth their lead warrior. From the back of Israel's infantry, David volunteers.

Here is a wiry, adolescent shepherd boy volunteering to take on the Philistine giant Goliath! It is thought that Goliath was almost eight feet tall and a trained combat fighter. Goliath has the advantage. But David did something simple yet remarkable. He did not succumb to the "presenting situations" rule. He realized his disadvantages (height, strength, lack of experience), but saw that they gave him an advantage. Since he was smaller, David knew he could move faster than Goliath. He also knew Goliath had poor vision, so staying at a distance was an advantage. Plus, David was a master with a slingshot. David chose not to play into his enemy's strengths. Instead, he chose to leverage his own advantages. He picked up a rock and launched it with his slingshot right to the head of the giant and killed him.

A second example of reframing advantages and disadvantages is how wealthy parents nowadays may be at a disadvantage in some respects. This is not suggesting by any stretch that being in poverty is somehow easy. Wealth provides opportunities for things like good education, better coaching in sports, social status, and access to better nutrition. Parents in poverty, on the other hand, have to struggle to get children adequate clothing and sports gear. They have fewer opportunities for education, less financial ability, and less access to nutrition. It is perceivable to make the judgment that wealthy parents hold an advantage in every way over parents in poverty.

However, parenting from a position of privilege presents a disadvantage. When children see resources (money) are at their immediate access, it is harder for parents to say, "no". It is difficult to hold the boundaries when children see access to significant resources in front of their eyes. Most of the time, parents give in to their children's requests. Privileged children often don't understand the value of work. If you don't earn it, you cannot intrinsically value it. However, children raised in settings of poverty understand the value of money and resources because they have to be earned. Therefore, parents who aren't wealthy have an easier time teaching responsibility. In that sense, wealthy parents have a disadvantage.

Five Agreements that Help Us Live into Deeper Meaning

1. Agree with yourself that your list of absolutes in life needs to shrink.
2. Agree that your weakness is here and you will not dismiss it. In the midst of it, find dependence on God. Identify what other strengths manifest themselves as a result of that weakness.
3. Agree that your contradictory behavior might need to exist in order to teach you something.
4. Agree that there is moral "gray area" that may be purposely present in your life, and that it is there to help you exist with others and yourself.
5. Agree that depending on God is your strongest method of coping with tension.

We find breath in being able to reframe our lives. It is NOT easy. I never want to imply that. To say reframing is easy is like saying that once you get your driver's license you become a skilled F-1 driver (see how I used a metaphor to frame that?). Reframing our struggles and weaknesses takes time, careful attention, and help. Essentially, what we try to accomplish is the art of molding our thoughts and perspectives into a view that makes sense. But it can be hard to do that on our own. I truly believe this is where skilled therapists come into play. It can be of great value to step out and ask for help. A therapist can help you to consider perspectives you may not have thought of on your own by pointing you toward a new lens to look through. It's our chance at "magic."

We glean much from this method of "magic," of pictures from metaphors, of unwinding distorted thoughts, of understanding tension's value, and of finding meaning in paradoxes. It's a gift God offers us—to find vision where we were once blind. I spent a lot of time discussing the power of reframing because it is so essential. I mean, what would life be like if all we did was look at our situation and conclude, "Well, this is how it is; there's nothing I can do." We might be doomed to have no faith at all. There would not be art in the world because we would all be confined to seeing life only one way.

But, as the Creator, as the ultimate artist, God designed us and the world with many lenses we can look through. There are new ways for us to look at our weaknesses, our relationships, our disadvantages, what we lack in our life, etc. This does require work and people who can help us find vision. The blind man did not find sight on his own; he had help. This is one of the purposes of counseling.

The Practice of Mindset Transformation

Make a commitment to yourself to find more than one way to look at your situation.

1. Look for what is currently presenting trouble in your life that might benefit from reframing.
2. Identify a strength from a suffering that might be trying to emerge.
3. Identify a metaphor fits and helps you with a challenging situation.
4. Focus for three minutes on what you have, not what you don't have.
5. Focus on what is in your control versus what is out of your control.
6. Give this current situation a new meaning.
7. Act on something you can you do now that will serve a higher purpose.

More Practice in Gaining Vision

1. Observe the story of the two men on the road to Emmaus (Luke 24:13-35). Two men come upon a stranger and begin conversing about the death of Jesus. The stranger,

Jesus, was seen by them yet not recognized. It's not until they sit and eat with him that they recognize it's Jesus. I want you to observe all the major parts and events of your daily and weekly life. Try and see where you recognize more than what meets the eye. It could be that you recognize something grand, spiritual, or God-like. Take note, and when you do recognize something, acknowledge it and interact with it. Further, can you look closer in your day to day living and identify where God's spirit or presence of Christ was right with you, but you did not notice it at first?

2. In reflecting on a time of struggle, darkness, tragedy, or trauma somewhere in your life, I want you to see if you can recognize where there may be a blessing or growth from that event/moment. If you can, recognize a strength that came from it. Much of what we learn we end up wishing we never knew. But it doesn't mean it is without value. Look carefully and try to identify the strength and blessing from such a tragic time/event.

3. We can relate, I hope, to having an experience that seemed small but held profound meaning. These situations often fall under the category of cute or sentimental or nice. Observe something that appears small—but then make it grand, and attempt to find some pattern of God in it. Take, for example, the sunrise. It is a regular occurrence and it is expected. But if you take the time to reflect, the sunrise can hold deep meaning. The start of something can be renewal. Renewal is like forgiveness, and forgiveness adds life. The sun adds more and more warmth as it rises. The sounds of birds increase along with the rays of sun. The sun gives life, just like the Son of God brings life out of death. All that from a sunrise. Find your small but big moment in the next 24 hours.

4. Identify one of your disadvantages or weaknesses. How is that weakness perfecting strength in you? How is that creating deeper reliance on God and others? How is that developing you as a person?

5. What is challenging or overwhelming in your life right now? As I mentioned before, pick a metaphor that resonates with you and apply it to your situation. Spend some time with that. Sit with it. And then recognize how you now feel about that situation.
6. Was there a time in your life where you experienced the principles discussed in the "Silver Medal" section? Are you stuck with the defeat of coming in second? Or can you find value in the process? Are you caught in the trap of comparing yourself to others? We are comparative creatures—it's in our DNA. We compare ourselves with others, whether about careers, appearances, successes, progress, homes, cars, education, etc. We compare all the time. And if we are honest, what is the most prevalent feeling as a result of comparing? Usually, we don't measure up and that feels condemning. We cut ourselves down for not living up. And when we compare and think we are ahead, does that really help? Does it really serve us to say, "Yes, I am doing better than so and so?" It is our ego that takes in that short saccharine sugar burst of a winning comparison. The great Dr. Jordan Peterson has said many times, "Compare yourself to who you were yesterday, last week, last month, or last year. You are the only one you can accurately compare yourself with anyway."

It is such a gift to realize we can look at life through many lenses. We are not imprisoned to the surface meanings of our situations. We are not locked into how culture says things are meant to be. We are not chained to limited perspectives that do nothing but take away our breath.

KEITH HUGHES, M.A.

Closing Prayer – Reprise

Lord, high and holy, meek and lowly. You have brought me to the valley of vision, where I live in the depths but see you in the heights; hemmed in by mountains of sin I behold your glory. Let me learn by paradox that the way down is the way up, that to be low is to be high, that the broken heart is the healed heart, that the contrite spirit is the rejoicing spirit, that the repenting soul is the victorious soul, that to have nothing is to possess all, that to bear the cross is to wear the crown, that to give is to receive, that the valley is the place of vision. Lord, in the daytime stars can be seen from deepest wells, and the deeper the wells the brighter your stars shine; let me find your light in my darkness, your life in my death, your joy in my sorrow, your grace in my sin, your riches in my poverty, your glory in my valley. Amen.

THE WORSHIP CODE

It's not that you don't worship, but it's what you worship.
Good Things Should Not Become Ultimate Things

WHEN IS ENOUGH, enough? Ponder that question over almost anything in your life. When is there enough money? When is there enough attention? When is there enough validation? How much is enough safety and control? How much power is enough? When is there enough until you are happy? When is there enough 'likes' on our social media pages? Answering those questions can be elusive, and difficult. The meaning of the word, 'enough' has a density to it because it points to the deeper issue of satisfaction or contentment. Discerning what is 'enough' of anything in life is what determines fulfillment or dissatisfaction. The disparity between what we have and what we think we need or want determines contentment or unhappiness. The real danger is when too much is not enough. That is when your soul has been taken over by disordered desire. In other words, when we don't know when it is "enough" of a finite thing then that 'thing' becomes the thing we serve and even worship.

Without contentment, our lives manifest states of insatiable desires, compulsivity, emptiness, greed, and unfulfilled lives. In other words, it is a dangerous place to be when *too much is not enough*. We live in a culture that seems to breed the mentality that we can never have enough of anything. The inability to find contentment causes the aforementioned situations. Further, not having some level of contentment in life can cause us to make simply good things, into ultimate things. I should note, however, that being content is not in competition with ambition. It is when content is pushed aside so that we might try to obtain more of what we 'want' versus what we need. Or we chase things down with such fury, that our thirst is never quenched. This causes us to become unhealthily attached or obsessed with something or someone and becomes an ultimate presence in our lives. Again, it is when we make a good thing into an ultimate thing, that 'thing' (person, entity, feeling) takes on an idol-like presence in us. And the nature of serving idols is that ultimately they imprison us, crush us if we don't crush it.

Too often I notice a major culprit in my clinical work is people mired in discontent. This results in lives out of balance from something becoming too centralized in their mind and soul. And that 'something' is not able to sustain necessary sanity in one's life. And the thing being chased down begins to take on a god-like quality. This is where the concept of worship comes into play, or inadequate worship, when we might have an insufficient thing that defines our being, our core our north. Deciding upon one's north, one's ultimate, deserves close evaluation. If not looked into closely, that 'thing' being chased down and bowed to will take one's breath away.

This breath of life has to do with a code in the world that I call the worship code. One of my purposes as a therapist is to help people identify patterns in their lives. This means looking at patterns of behavior, thought, and feelings, in addition, to evaluating intentional things like traditions, routines, rituals, and habits. When we evaluate healthy and unhealthy patterns of living, we must ask why they exist and how to alter or rearrange them so that life can be manageable and understandable. Specifically, the patterns I am speaking of lead to addictions, sabotage, relational failure, mood disorders, and spiritual ambiguity. A significant amount of work in my clinical practice addresses the practice of worship.

4 Breaths

Living in this Western culture, it is nearly impossible not to come upon some kind of iconic entity or being. We live in a culture that has an insatiable desire to worship the next best thing. Our culture is saturated with gods that represent all aspects of modern civilization. It seems we cannot just allow things to "be" just what they are. We need to elevate things to be "iconic," "epic," "idol," "the greatest," "the most ___," or "number 1." We keep creating, nominating, titling, and proclaiming who is or what is the greatest.

We see it in sports, sports athletes, celebrities, fashion, power, sex, beauty, entertainment, business, education, recreation, politics, and social media. We see it all over the place, especially at the end or beginning of the year we see a plethora of 'lists' ranking 'the best', 'the number 1', the 'most', etc. We love to rank anything we can. That to me is an interesting phenomenon. I can't help but see that pointing toward our need for 'the ultimate', 'the idol'. We can't help ourselves, we need to exalt. And it's not a secret. One of the most successful (and original) singing reality shows was "American Idol." The blatant confession by the industry and culture is "We idolize our entertainers, so come on down and line up to be the next 'American Idol.'" The pursuit of God is sometimes found in our worship of things that we find are right in front of us.

The worship code. I'd simply put it this way: there is a broader social code of worship or pattern of behavior. When I say worship, I look at it as having two levels. Cheering and exalting some entity like an entertainer or sports figure could be categorically and arguably be called worship. But, for the purposes here, the deeper level of worship I am identifying is when something gets a hold of our being, our spirit, which becomes so central in us that we look to "it" as a god of some sort.

This kind of inner arrangement and behavior is driven by an instinctual need to exalt, edify, and bow down to something bigger than ourselves. To fill in the God-shaped hole in our souls. Our feverish pursuit of things to exalt speaks to a deep yearning in our souls to find life, energy, purpose, and identity. There is a significant amount of breath we receive in worshiping. This urge for worship is also correlated to our internal innate desires. It's when our innate desires fall into unhealthy modes of gaining fulfillment that they become disordered patterns—or, disordered desires. *Making a good (finite) thing turn into the ultimate* object of our affection leads us to a soul-sucking trap.

I know that the word "worship" can seem irrelevant if you're not from a religious background. But stay with me here, because if we are honest with ourselves, the idea of worship is not a foreign idea to you whatsoever. The idea of exalting a person, thing, or ideology beyond what it was meant to be is blatantly manifested in our world. We live in a "hype" culture—or better stated, an "idol culture." The impact it has on our outlook, mental health, and spirit is riveting.

This chapter's purpose is to illuminate the concept of how our desires become disordered and create impossible idols in our lives, thus creating unhealthy circumstances that rot us from the inside out. Worshipping something that cannot sustain the center of your soul/life will only take your breath away (in a bad way). Furthermore, when I say, "rot us from the inside out," I specifically mean how our lives become problematic to the point of being emotionally, physically, and spiritually bankrupt. It's one of those things that's staring at us all the time, but we don't talk about it. It surrounds us 24/7. By "it" I mean the exaltation of any person, ideology, being, or thing. Whenever something suggests that it will help us feel significant, loved, safe, or excited, we are tempted to bow to it in hopes that it will fix our empty, small, mundane lives. We know this to be true. We cannot help but follow the vapor trails of hype. The idea of having an idol is the norm.

One might think, "So what is the problem with having idols? Isn't it harmless? Unless you're religious, why would it matter?" Ironically, most people take no issue with the order of life that the Ten Commandments outline. Most civilizations can agree to not murder, steal, or take another man's wife, honor your mother and father, and don't covet. But the command of "have no other false gods before me" seems easily passed over. We love our idols. Here is the point, there seems to be an inner design of humanity that compels us to place something into the center of our life, heart, or soul. And this thing we place in the center (the idol), we look to it to give us safety, flourishing, advancement, fulfillment, meaning, purpose, love, etc. It is unavoidable. We all do it. The issues, what we place in the center of our life like and idol or "God" is what makes all the difference. Is your idol/God sustainable for your whole life? That is what is at hand here. Whether one is religious or not. This is how I look into the meaning of this 'commandment'. Besides God being a God who desires to be loved by His creation and nobody else to be loved above Him, He knows nothing else can sustain your life like Him, on earth and in eternity.

Here is something peculiar. If you ever take a close look into the Bible, specifically the Old Testament, there are all kinds of violations of the Ten Commandments, and God is kind and merciful. He forgives adultery, murder, stealing, and lying. Just look at King David. He seduces and forces Bathsheba into an adulterous act. And then David murders her husband, who is also David's right-hand man in the army. What does God do then? He waits for David's repentance and forgives him. But when we see God's people put another god before Him and worship a carved image, He nearly *loses his last nerve*, boiling in wrath to the point that He gets close to eliminating His people. He is *enraged* to the point of death**.** Having an idol in front of God is a big offense and seems like a big deal. I will once again, reiterate this in two ways. God, naturally, wants no other God worshipped before him, because He is The Lord of all. Second, His design in life is that anything else we put in the center of our life simply doesn't work as well as having Him central in our life.

Like most things in life, there is a spectrum, a degree by which things become disordered. On one end, you can have a life of stress and moderate chaos. Or the other extreme, you can have a deep addiction. Disordered desires that manifest a behavioral pattern, or even addiction, expose the reality that we all worship something. This worship pattern is so prominent in our world that a non-religious, gnostic author and philosopher, David Foster Wallace, made this profound observation:

David Foster Wallace

> *Because here's something else that's weird but true: in the day-to-day trenches of adult life, there is actually no such thing as atheism. There is no such thing as not worshipping. Everybody worships. The only choice we get is what to worship.*
>
> *And the compelling reason for maybe choosing some sort of god or spiritual-type thing to worship—be it JC or Allah, be it YHWH or the Wiccan Mother Goddess, or the Four Noble Truths, or some inviolable set of ethical principles—is that pretty much anything else you worship will eat you alive.*
>
> *If you worship money and things, if they are where you tap real meaning in life, then you will never have enough, never feel you have enough. It's the truth. Worship your body and beauty and sexual allure and you will always feel ugly. And when time and age start showing, you will die a million deaths before they finally grieve you. On one level, we all know this stuff already. It's been codified as myths, proverbs, clichés, epigrams, parables, the skeleton of every great story. The whole trick is keeping the truth up front in daily consciousness.*
>
> *Worship power, you will end up feeling weak and afraid, and you will need ever more power over others to numb you to your own fear. Worship your intellect, being seen as smart, you will end up feeling stupid, a fraud, always on the verge of being found out. But the insidious thing about these forms of worship is not that they're evil or sinful, it's that they're unconscious. They are default settings.* (David Foster Wallace, "A Different Kind of Freedom," 3/7/2010, accessed 9/15/2023)

Mr. Wallace makes an astute observation. We all worship something, and *what* we worship makes all the difference. I can 100% attest from the long length of my work that clients often wonder, "What's the reason for my collapse?" After sifting through the rubble, we begin to discover one of the major factors that led to that individual falling down. What we discover is there was something that had become central in their life that could not sustain them. I say "central" because within each individual is a "center"—whether we call it soul, spirit, or "God-shaped hole." How we go about filling that space is crucial. Addictions, I think, are one of the best analogies to describe this process/phenomenon. After the introduction of any addictive substance, that substance becomes the centerpiece of the person's life. As the addiction takes residence in someone, most aspects of his or her life become tainted, impacted, and robbed by the addiction. The addiction is centralized, causing the mind, body, and spirit of a person to become enthralled by what the substance creates. Again, *too much is not enough*.

Why Do We Worship?

By the patterned nature of living, we see there is a *need* to have something ultimate before us. Therefore, we all worship something because we *need* to. It is in the DNA of our being to worship. We have a system of needs in us that drives us to fulfill needs for significance, love, growth, and security. And what or who we worship is part of how we get those needs fulfilled. What and how we worship also speaks to who we are and want to become more alike.

There is a saying, "we become what we worship". And for the most part, I tend to agree that the premise seems accurate. What we worship, is our way of saying we agree and identify with that entity. We find it to have ultimate worth and it deserves exaltation. Our worship toward something also says I want to be more like that and want to be defined by that. Therefore, what we worship can make a difference in the trajectory of our lives. This seems to naturally speak to the great design of God, that by worshipping Him, in praise and service, we are aligning ourselves with the essence, qualities, heart, and character of God. And it is God, the creator of life, our bodies, soul, and mind, who can touch upon and fulfill the breadth, width, and depth of our needs.

Further, we order our lives by a compass; internal and external. I live in Colorado, so we have this natural compass that orders our directions and bearings. Just look for the mountains, and then North is easy to find. Left. We live our lives by markers for directions, distance, and time. We also have an internal compass. This might be identified as our soul. The ever-encompassing part of us that holds our essence, instincts, drive, and desires. Utilizing our soul for direction is what we do whether we are conscious of it or not. Simply when we notice our desires and what feeds them, we understand the direction we are taking in life. And here is when life gets off course, we can lose direction. When desires in us get 'out of order' life gets out of order, and good things become ultimate.

The Core of What We Need

Disordered desires can happen when we try to meet our needs in an unhealthy way. The psychological theory here is that needs drive desire, and desire drives behavior. How we manage our needs makes all the difference. In this following section, I am adopting some ideas from the great Tony Robbins. Here are some of our core needs and how they are related to our desires. Once again, it is our desires that point us toward our actions and are what pull good things into the center of our lives and make them ultimate things.

Certainty – Our need for order, control, and safety. This need is what we have that keeps us from pain. To the degree we need distance from pain or discomfort, we will work diligently to exercise control, safety, and order. Now the strategy by which we meet our certainty/control need can make all the difference in how we relate to others and the world at large. We either have a functioning, healthy, and reasonable strategy for "certainty" or we can choose to fall into non-productive, destructive, intrusive, abusive, and aggressive strategies for Certainty. How we negotiate our control needs with the world makes a big difference. For instance, a quick and easy default for finding certainty and order from pain is anger. Think about it, when something occurs out of our control and poses any kind of physical, or emotional threat, we lash out in heated anger to restore order. Anger can be an effective emotion sometimes to assert our will over or into something. But if you're a raging adult in the world, you ironically may find your anger creating irony by creating pain in your existence.

Potential Disordered Desires: Anger Mismanagement, OCD, Assorted Phobias, Control issues, Anxiety, Substance Abuse.

Productive Strategies: Prayer, meditation, mindfulness, radical acceptance or agreeability.

Variance – The real need for unknowns, change, variety and excitement. This need is the opposite sibling of "certainty" as it is what drives one to need change and adventure in life. Like certainty, people have a different degree of need for variance. Our need for variety is also core to us. Because, like certainty, where we need some sense of life having order and safety, there is a real need for variety. The variety needs helps us continue to grow and to combat plateauing in our development. Some who have strong needs for variance display a 'thrill seeker' side of life while on the other side of the spectrum, we find persons/personalities who feel they thrive well on routine, predictability, etc. It might be summarized that each extreme presents its own potential disordered desires:

Potential Disordered Desires: Adrenaline junkies, relationship breakers, boredom, lack of growth due to lack of risk or change; laziness; inability to for regularity

Productive Strategies: Planned change. Re-order your schedule. Measured risk-taking.

Significance – *To know how much we are valued and need meaning and purpose.* This need presents itself in therapy sessions frequently. As in, struggling to feel or find oneself as significant. I might say this need, and Love, are the most pronounced in my discussions with clients. The pursuit of significance seems to present the most trouble in people's lives, second to love. It's not a secret that much has been written over the centuries about significance. Probably since the beginning of time, the human need for meaning and purpose has been sought after. Significance drives us in various ways. In my work with people, the strategies to fulfill this need are profoundly inspiring and at times devastatingly shameful. We can go to great lengths in life to find out how our life matters, and what it means. We all want to know we have worth and value. Self-worth is a prolific quest in our world. I have witnessed how we will go in absorbent amounts of debt, monetarily, and psychologically to experience tangible ways we are significant to others and ourselves. Whether that means we join a particular social group or a relationship, join a movement of religious or social justice, write a book (LOL), create art, or spiritual quests, play sports, or push our limitations to see how ultimately we can accomplish specific feats. I mean, the list goes on and on in how we try to pursue significance and meaning and purpose in life. Again, the strategy for significance demands careful strategy because all too much I have seen that if the strategy for significance is not with good discernment, destruction and poor compromise occur.

The Disordered Desires for significance can be: Inappropriate need for power, arrogance, false humility, over committed and burn out. Depression. Ego Personality Disorders

Productive Strategies: Participate in a healthy spiritual community. Worship services. Volunteer and serve. Practice vulnerability in a relationship. Choose a career over a job. Listen more than you speak. Pray and meditate.

Love – The famous need that enthralls the mind, heart, and soul. Probably the most obvious of needs. But love is easily the leader of reasons why many if not most, enter into therapy. Seeking help with troubled relationships (married/dating/siblings) being unable to find love, or not feeling love from a spouse, friends, or family. Not being loved, or able to receive love due to specific reasons (trauma, abandonment) creates one of the leaders of death in the world, loneliness. Contending with loneliness can be quite a war. The power of love and the need for it has led many of us into the abyss of failure, frustration, and grand attempts that led us to be broke and empty. Selling out one's soul is a practice all too many have committed. Not trying to be too dramatic, but not far from the truth, we will do just about anything for love; just research every other love song and we hear this. We just might sell our heart or soul for love by that one who captivated us. And once we have found love, one of the most written about ideas is 'how do we make love stay?'. This is also the title of a popular Dan Fogelberg song in the 1980s, "How Do We Make Love Stay?" How do we find it? How can we receive it? How do we keep it? And how we go about all of those journeys is deserving of deep exploration and careful discernment.

Disordered Desires: Depression. Love addiction. Lust. Sex addiction. Pornography addiction. Co-Dependency patterns. Apocalyptic expectations

Productive Strategies: Vulnerability. Avoid apocalyptic expectations. Humility. Vulnerability is accomplished by courage; and boundaries.

Growth – Experience learning, expanding, and accomplishing. This is the need that I see show up in people's lives who experience plateauing, boredom, and an overall sense of feeling stuck. This is the need in us that needs to experience growth in knowledge, character, understanding, and overall development. Growing is in the DNA of existence. Since the moment we are born we "grow" physically, cognitively, emotionally, etc. We may physically stop growing at age 19 but the rest of us have a degree of need to grow in all the other areas. The principle of growing is essential as evidenced in the business mantra we hear that exhorts by saying "if you're not growing, you're dying". And that mantra holds some fundamental truth. When we stop growing, there is some form of death that goes on in us when we are not learning, changing, and evolving with our environment. The lack of growth can be equated with the process we call atrophy. If we are not growing, atrophy in different areas of our life can occur and that is a certain kind of death, indeed.

Disordered Desires: avoidance strategies, phobias, settling, low self-worth; greed; pride.

Productive Strategies: valuing slow growth; valuing risk-taking; valuing learning.

Contribute – the need to serve or give toward the system, relationship, grouping or society to which you belong. We all have a core need to give toward what we belong. The lack of this need being met/exercised can result in taking a hit on one's worth, identity, and purpose. Being able to contribute toward something is a way we validate the world around us, and validate the resources within us, which helps our sense of self-worth and purpose. When we feel like we have nothing to offer in a relationship, our work, our community, we can be at risk of feeling unsure of our worth.

Disordered Desires: work addiction

Productive Strategies: Find clear ways to help, serve, give; ask our world what it needs. Be diligent and intentional; Find balance.

Energy – we all have our own energy needs. This is regarding the temperament need of extraversion and introversion needs. I found that lacking awareness of this need brings about much havoc. Not being aware of one's energy reserves and social styles can get in the way of functioning.

We are either walking toward order or we are uncorking chaos. If what we worship is unable to handle our needs, it will eventually crumble, and we will crumble with it. If we worship what is true and worthy, then we find a place of certainty in life. To put it plainly, if we worship God, then we will have order in life. The key principle here is we need to know what we are looking toward to accurately satiate our needs. Our existence in the day-to-day is our search to fulfill our needs. As mentioned earlier, being led by disordered desires is what creates unproductive and destructive behaviors. Here is an outline of our needs. Simply, by having an unsustainable thing at the core of our being, where we are trying to find certainty, love, and significance, then that thing will take your breath away. But if we seek to have the highest possible good, thing, entity, and God at the center, then our soul will breathe with infinite energy.

When something finite becomes too important in our lives we get out of balance. I've seen this play out in a wide range of ways: A youth whose sanity is shaken by achieving a 4.0 GPA instead of a 4.5; an anxiety-ridden adult who cannot sleep, rest, or be at peace because in his head he creates fictional problematic scenarios; the alcohol-addicted executive; the porn-addicted youth that will stay up until 4 am to break a computer filter. The consistent question that arises is "Why do I do this? Why can't I stop?" Why can't any of us stop? Why can't we stop our patterned behavior of centralizing things that really cannot stay central in our lives?

This reminds me of a teenage girl I counseled. She was about 16 years old, extremely bright, focused, responsible, and conscientious. This young lady sat on the couch and explained what triggered the downward spiral of self-harm and not wanting to live anymore. We will call her "Kay." She quietly, calmly, and elaborately laid out her tale of the immense work she had put into her recent semester at school. Kay was an honors student with dreams of attending an Ivy League college school. However, all of that appeared to be in jeopardy. Kay was striving to bring her 4.0 GPA up closer to a 4.5, but she didn't get the 4.5. The "failure" of not reaching this GPA indicated to her that she was not enough, a failure, a fraud, and not a good person. The urge to die started to consume her. So, she began to harm herself and made an exit strategy to end her life. Yes, life and death hung in the balance of a few tenths of a GPA.

To the common observer, I know this appears extreme. But if you drill down deep into her story, it is not far from any of ours. When our career, love, friends, family, money, or hobbies are threatened, we feel the same empty and desperate ache. This young lady found her identity, worth, security, and importance in her grades. On the outside, it seems irrational, but if we are honest, we are all susceptible to a similar story. *"We try and find ourselves in ego-shaped roles that don't really affirm the best part of us. Our true self. Our true self, in simple terms, the Christ in us looking back at God"*. (Richard Rohr, 'Falling Upward' 2011)

More often than not, it's the beautiful things that we allow to become central in us. *But good things cannot become ultimate things.* Life has many fine lines—they are unseen yet profoundly real. There is a line between love and obsession, between desire and lust, between wanting something and hinging our life upon getting it, between anger and rage, between rest and sloth. There is a line we can cross that moves our life from order to chaos. Take some time to reflect on those times when things become too important in your life. How did that feel? Why did they rise to that high level of importance?

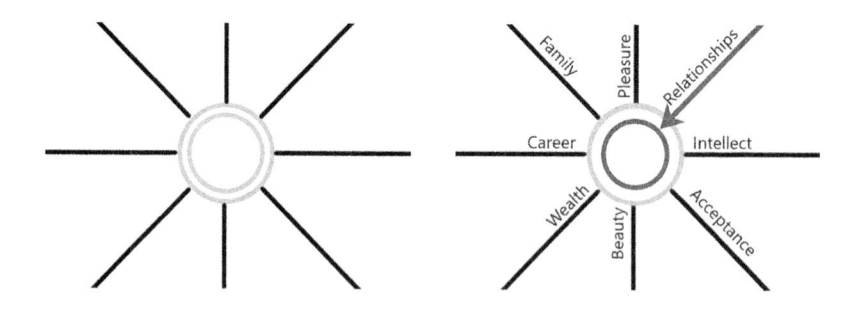

Finding the Breath of Worship

We all are designed to worship. We need to worship. It's an undeniable urge. Addressing the Worship Current

The worship wheel as seen above I have used this wheel extensively in classes/groups I lead to be a visual to the content of worship, and 'good becoming ultimate'. Each spoke around the circle is labeled by any good thing, entity, or content in your life.

The circle represents your soul or spirit, and I pose the question: "What might you choose that could be ultimate enough, dynamic, powerful, loving, and creative enough to be in the circle, and help substantially meet your needs?" This is where the spiritual aspect comes in. What is strong enough that can hold, sustain, and temper our desires? What can provide enough assurance in our lives that we don't have to compulsively control our world? What can give us the peace of mind that we can survive anything that comes our way? What gives us a sense of significance but doesn't force us to sell our souls? What tells you that you are truly loved? What is powerful enough to provide you with ultimate and eternal ways of growth? Without further ado; God. To most people, it's probably obvious as well. But honestly, this dilemma of worshipping things that are unfit to be worshiped happens to many believers. We all have seasons in which idols creep into the center of our souls. This is where the 'how' becomes so critical. How can we truly allow God to participate in the central part of our being? How do we make God the center of life? This seems like something we learned in youth bible camp, but, yet the lesson eludes us.

The Sermon on The Mount

I would like to point to the Sermon on the Mount. In Matthew 6, we read how Jesus gives a lesson on anxiety. Although he specifically addresses anxiety, he gives a model by which we can safeguard ourselves from worshipping counterfeit things. How this form of worship can combat anxiety.

> *"For this reason, I say to you, do not be worried about your life, as to what you will eat or what you will drink; nor for your body, as to what you will put on. Is not life more than food, and the body more than clothing? Look at the birds of the air, that they do not sow nor reap nor gather into barns, and yet your heavenly Father feeds them. Are you not worth more than they? … you worry what are we to wear? What are we to drink or eat? For*

your heavenly Father knows that you need all these things. And which of you by worrying can add a single day to his life's span? But seek first His Kingdom and His righteousness, and all these things will be added to you."
(Matthew 6:25-26, 32, 33-34 NASB 2020)

Jesus says to stop obsessively focusing on temporal needs. To redefine the essentials of life demands that we consider the infinite. Jesus points to the birds who trust God to feed them. If he feeds them, why wouldn't he feed you? We do not need to obsessively focus on the temporal and finite things. In verses 33-34, he directs his audience to seek the highest good—God's Kingdom and His righteousness. And what is the "Kingdom of God" exactly? It always intrigues me when I ask someone, what IS the Kingdom of God? Often, there is an awkward pause, a stressful stare, struggling to come up with the right words. And it should. The Kingdom of God is the highest possible thought to imagine and ponder. A starting point for understanding the Kingdom of God can begin with these: when we ponder God's way/ pattern, the depths of the universe, creation, heaven, and the afterlife. What is mercy, grace, love, order, redemption, righteousness, hope, eternal life, etc? How do evil, suffering, and sin exist in light of God?

These are parts of what comprises 'The Kingdom of God'. When we begin to ponder, seek, understand, and put into action, we automatically prioritize life in its proper order, and the temporal things of our life get into manageable perspective. Jordan Peterson says it well. 'When you are worried, stop and think about the highest most complex idea you can think of. Love, sure. Joy, sure. But what about God and His Kingdom? Try that!" When we look at our compass that way, we find north. And when you locate north, then you know how to proceed.

Setting our imagination on the highest possible good, the Kingdom of God, it does something to the mind. It widens our perspective. It connects us to the infinite God who cares for us. Putting our attention on something higher and better creates order within our life. We adore God rather than created things. We can put our focus on and trust in God so that the finite things can and will get fulfilled. Obsessively focusing on the temporal, finite things of life—food, people, money, status, career, etc.—will not sustain us long-term. When you focus on God and on your present moment, it's difficult to be anxious. And most likely we experience what is…*enough.*

Remember, we are all worshipers. And as we travel through life, we pick up wounds and disappointments, which we tend to address with something else besides God. When we are wounded or disappointed, we have to remember that Christ is the center of our lives. As Richard Rohr says, in "Falling Upward", "*We try and find ourselves in ego-shaped roles that don't really affirm the best part of us. Our true self. Our true self, in simple terms, is the Christ in us looking back at God. How are we getting a hold of the Christ in us? How do we find ourselves 'in Christ'?*" We worship.

Ways to Worship (preserving the center)

Meditation/prayer

1. The Meditation/Prayer: Each of these for 3 minutes

    - Deep Breathing – Wim Hoff Method, 4-6-4 (Inhale 4 seconds, hold 6, exhale 4 seconds)
    - Gratitude
    - Asking for help and visualizing that part of your healing
    - Blessing upon others in your life

2. The Practice of Awe: go somewhere; the ocean, before or on top of a high place or mountain, and just take in the beauty, the depth, the size, the distance of what is before you and how it was created. It was created by the breath of God. Express your gratitude to Him.
3. Regularly participate in worship/praise services and be mindful of words, phrases, and sounds that resonate with

your heart. Sing with your heart, don't worry about the notes. Sing, Sing, Sing!
4. Read about God. Learning about the depths of God helps keep God central in us. The Bible Project is a great on-line resource for podcasts and classes. www.bibleproject.com
5. Practice mindfulness activities that put you in the now (deep breathing, smell, use all senses)
6. Service. Serve where it costs you something. Meaning, where it puts you out of your comfort zone. Where only others benefit from your service.
7. Be in a like-minded community for connection (to be loved, to contribute)
8. The practice of daily, intentional gratitude every day for 3 minutes or more.
9. Participate in nearly anything in the arts that you have an affinity towards music, dance, painting, drawing, writing, etc.

Closing Words

Worship. It is what we do. As David Foster Wallace pointed out, it is what we worship that makes all the difference. We tend to lose our breath, and our life, when we allow a finite, temporal, and superficial entity to take the center of our soul. When we try and find ourselves in something that will not sustain us, we run into trouble—whether that's an addiction, imbalance, devastation, or disappointment. What gives us breath is when our life is ordered around God and his priorities. The regular practice of worshipping God lends us a knowledge of what is ultimate and what is good. And by that, the things we love in life learn their proper place and meaning. So we go on and worship. I encourage you to find your breath daily. Keep your aim on the ultimate of life. Be watchful that desires don't become inflamed—because they easily do. Worship God regularly so that you can maintain a workable perspective on life.

MASHALEM "IT IS FINISHED" PART I

ירושלים

Breaths from The Cross

"You turned shame into glory"

LIFE IS LIKE a crucifixion or at least feels like it. We all try to endure this slow crucifixion as we fall, doing things that make the pain of life all that more unbearable. Before we know it, we feel discouraged, beaten down and ashamed. Embarrassed by what or who we have become, as shame intoxicates us, accusing us of how wretched we have become. Creating in us a ticking time bomb.

So how do you dismantle this atomic bomb? The deconstruction of guilt and shame is like dismantling an atomic bomb. Both can be quite complicated, and dangerous, even life and death. Bombs kill human beings, and shame kills souls. When we address shame, it demands our careful attention, because how shame shapes our emotional and psychological foundations can create easy access to explosive emotions. Shame sucks the breath out of the lungs of our soul. But we are afforded the Cross and the meaning of Jesus's cross as something that gives us breath and oxygen to inhale.

This is not a singular comprehensive narrative in addressing shame. However, I want to look at this condition and the greater condition of sin through the lens of Jesus' crucifixion. Arguably the most impactful moment in history is Jesus' death on the Cross and his resurrection three days later. Through careful observance of the crucifixion, I want to highlight the overt and covert messages coming from this historical, spiritual, and transcendent event. The Cross and resurrection have produced specific Christian theologies, which I will unpack. However, the Cross also addresses shame and guilt. And it has a way to combat the thoughts of shame and guilt, dismantling the atomic impact they have on us. And, again, looking at the cross as a means of filling our soul with breath.

The psychology of the Cross displays to us how the ultimate, perfect being of Jesus demonstrates complete empathy and becomes the guilty one by becoming the very thing that shames us. The hero levels the playing field and takes on the worst in order to heal us. He takes the blame and eternal consequences for our failures. By becoming sin, not only does Jesus understand it, but he holds complete understanding of shame and guilt. The great irony is He didn't commit any moral, social, or political crime, but a religious crime; proclaiming to be the Son of Man. He was found guilty. Talk about injustice!

Mashalem! Those are the final words of Jesus. *Mashalem* is Aramaic for "it is finished." The Greek translation for "it is finished" which is commonly referred to, is "tetelestai". Three words. Three important words that deserve some careful attention. I want to observe, absorb, and speak to the meaning of the Cross and *Mashalem*. Images and posters do not completely or accurately capture the actual agony and humiliation of what Jesus went through on the Cross. One may wonder: How does this fit into the scheme of mental health? Simply, I want to uncover how "Mashalem", in Christ's last and dying breath, he gave us a breath so we might have infinite life.

As mentioned above, addressing guilt and shame is a big task. Just hearing the words "guilt and shame" usually brings an immediate blow to the heart. We have all had our dose of guilt, shame, or both, delivered by the things we have done or the things others have done to us. As a result, they are cancers of the heart and soul, robbing us of our breath. Shame tells us we are bad, wrong, and unworthy of what is good and right in life. Guilt is the deep regret of an act we committed, imprisoning us to a jail cell of contempt, self-loathing, and self-hate. Shame within us demands treatment. Treating these conditions leads us to the Cross, for the Cross deals with sin, which in Greek, is *harmatia*. And shame is entwined with sin. As mentioned, shame is a soul cancer, but it is a treatable condition.

I hope to make the connections for us in how Jesus on the Cross addresses sin and shame. We can find breath by listening to the Cross. My hope is that you will sit well with the following understanding of sin, shame, and guilt. Because Jesus says the power of such things "is finished."

Breath is simply a metaphorical way of describing the maintenance and edification of our psychological and spiritual health. So, why the Cross? The Cross has held its sacred, definitive meaning for the Christian faith. Jesus sacrificed his life for the sins of all mankind. But what I am arguing is that the whole event and theology of Jesus' crucifixion is, rightly understood, a means to improve mental health. There is an application from it that can help us love our life and help negotiate through life. What occurred on the Cross is arguably the ultimate act in history. It demands reasonable understanding. It is unreasonable for us to overlook our potential or existing attachment to it.

The Cross has become an iconic symbol in the world. Even to the word, iconic, does not serve its prominence and meaning in the world. Ever since its inception, around 6 B.C. used by the Persians. Alexander the Great brought it from there to the eastern Mediterranean countries in the 4th Century B.C. and the Phoenicians introduced it to Rome in the 3rd Century B.C. It was used as an execution tool. The Romans perfected crucifixion for 500 years until it was abolished by Constantine I in the 4th century AD. Crucifixion in Roman times was applied mostly to slaves, disgraced soldiers, Christians and foreigners--only very rarely to Roman citizens. Death, usually after 6 hours--4 days, was due to multifactorial pathology: after-effects of compulsory scourging and maiming, hemorrhage and dehydration causing hypovolemic shock and pain, but the most important factor was progressive asphyxia caused by impairment of respiratory movement.

Since the 4th Century, it has been a religious symbol found in countless situations, used for myriads of reasons. Probably right at this moment as you are reading this, there is a human canvas being inked by a tattoo needle engraving the image of the cross. It's being placed on a wall somewhere: cathedral, church, office, a home, a sign. More peculiar, we find the image in the most unlikely places: heavy metal concerts and t-shirts, around the neck of a rock/pop artist. I am always intrigued by this, how the cross is displayed in the most secular places. It's captivating. I know for many this is sort of sac-religious. However, I think it says something.

The cross elicits so many things for people, as it should. Perhaps for the less religious, the cross represents sacrifice, pain, violence, death, grief, and loss. Its universal significance is not missed on humanity even if the meaning is unclear to some. The cross seems to be found just about anywhere/everywhere. I appreciate how the cross is elevated in the world from one extreme to another: bowed to on a Sunday morning, placed on top of heavenly cathedrals, sticking to a sweaty neck in a heavy metal show. It finds its place everywhere.

I'll repeat, not considering the Cross may be a grave oversight when considering the essentials of understanding spiritual living.

To me, it demands that we gaze upon it and consider it. I want to be clear: when referring to "the Cross" I am talking about the Cross WITH the dying Jesus on it.

What prompted me to unpack this here are two experiences. One, for 10 years I had the distinct honor and at times immense humbling experience to portray Jesus in the local, now international, production called the *Passion Play of Denver*. Portraying—rather, attempting to portray—Jesus on the Cross brought some transcending moments that I've never previously shared with anybody. And second, the articulate, mystic writing of Mr. Richard Rohr in *The Universal Christ* presented a piece of literature about the "message from the Cross" that has helped shape my view of the Crucifixion.

Observations of (from) the Cross

"One Night on the cross"

In some of my sessions or classes, I like to share a trivial fact about myself as an ice breaker. I say to people, "I have died over 88 times and came back to life." It usually elicits a shocking response until I explain I was blessed with the rare opportunity of playing Jesus in the annual *Passion Play of Denver* for 10 years.

There is an ocean-like depth of learning and development that occurred during this endeavor. Attempting to grasp the omnipotent love and eternal heart of Jesus is indescribable. I want to share one shocking observation. One night, while portraying Jesus in the *Passion Play of Denver*, the cross was hoisted up and into its slot. It slid down, slamming onto the ground. The crowd cheered and gazed at the scourged body and crown of thorns piercing into the skull. At that point, Mother Mary, John, and Peter approach. I am there, looking down, taking it in, and trying to express the agony Jesus must have gone through… The transcendence of acting is that you are afforded the opportunity to let yourself be in the character and the story, yet in the present time. At that moment, I was attempting to comprehend "being in" Jesus as he was crushed on the Cross. Right when the Cross settles in its spot, it hits me! And it was unbearable.

What overwhelmed me was the urge to cry out, "I AM SO SORRY!!!" I was dumbfounded. What does "sorry" mean? I felt this altered sense of repentant compassion—a breaking-down feeling. I felt an apocalyptic, cosmic sense of God trying to channel a multi-dimensional sentiment about His heart breaking over what His creation has endured. And in further thought the sentiment was just a sense of Jesus' breaking under the weight of compassion. The weight of the brokenness of the world pressing down on his heart and tortured body.

At that moment, I felt this sense that God through Jesus might be trying to say, among many other things, like after the Flood we hear God is sorry he even made mankind. I felt Him saying, "I am so sorry you had to go through all of this, that we had to endure this, and that right now you have to see me go through this! I will now take on your sin, your faults, your transgressions, and become your sin. Sins accusation is mine, never yours. I will become the worst thing possible. I will be your shame, your despicable self, your guilt, and your pain. The power of it is no longer. The Father and I agreed the power of it all is defeated right here, so I will take on the separateness between you and eternity, watch and wait as I kill death."

By taking on the sacrifice for mankind, it can be looked upon as taking responsibility, and with responsibility comes an act of confession. If one chooses to be guilty, it means he or she is taking on the blame. On the Cross, God takes on an apologetic tone. This is just one of the many statements the Cross makes.

A Biblical Account

Found not guilty by the Roman Pontiff (Luke 23:4,14,15, 22 NASB 2020) New American Standard 2020) "*Then*

Pilate said to the chief priests and the crowds, "I find not guilt in this man… why, what evil has this man done? I have found in Him no guilt demanding death."

Chosen over a murderer by the crowd (Luke 23:23-25 NASB 2020) *"But they were insistent, with loud voices asking that He be crucified. And their voices began to prevail. And Pilate pronounced sentence be granted. And he released the man they were asking for who had been thrown into prison for insurrection and murder, but he delivered Jesus to their will."*

Extreme torture (physical trauma)

He ministered and cared for family: (John 19:26 NASB 2020) "When Jesus then saw His mother, and the disciple whom He loved standing by He said to his mother "Woman behold your son!" Then He said… "John behold your mother"… "from that hour the disciple took her into his own household".

He offered redemption and salvation while in agony (Luke 23:43 NASB 2020) To the thief he says, *"Truly I say to you, today you shall be with Me in Paradise"*

Received mockery and hatred (Matthew 27:29 NASB 2020) *"And after twisting together a crown of thorns theu put it on his head… and they knelt down before him and mocked him"*

Offered forgiveness/compassion (Luke 23:34 NASAB 2020) *"Father forgive them, for they do not know what they do"*

Separated and forsaken from his father for the first Mark 15:34 time (emotional trauma) "My God, My God, why have you forsaken me?!"

Drank the sour wine, perhaps as a metaphorical toast (John 19:28-30) *"I am thirsty". A jar of sour wine was standing there… they brought it to his mouth… when he received the sour wine, He said, Into your hands I commend my spirit. "MASHALEM. It is finished"*

The blood spills out from Jesus—just like the traditional blood sacrifices done by the Jews in order to cleanse the individual and the community of their transgressions. It was a sacrament established by God and the nation of Israel that blood be spilled from a clean animal in order to cleanse the sins of the people. Blood represents life and the sacrifice and spilling of life redeems one's current life. So, we now see Jesus being sacrificed once and for all for all mankind; he is the living sacrifice bleeding and dying for the world's transgressions.

By this act, we have the vertical direction of the cross established. The power of sin, which separates us from God, has now been eliminated through the spilling of Jesus' blood. At the very moment this occurs, we see this manifested by Jesus' cry: "My God! My God! Why have you forsaken me?!" *For a long time, this has been interpreted to mean that Jesus is experiencing a first-time separation from His father.* By becoming sin, he was separated from God. On all of creation's behalf, he became the ultimate "sin".

Now we start to see the message reveal itself. We now see the sacrificed Jesus becoming the worst of all of creation (sin) on behalf of others. As Galatians 3:13 says, "He became a curse"—separating himself from his Father for the first time, like a cosmic divorce.

At this point, what can we understand from this visual of Jesus on the cross? What are the things He understands as it relates to the rest of humanity? God as man takes on and becomes intimate with suffering—with pain, loneliness, imperfection, sin, shame, guilt, sorrow, torture, violence. There, up on the Cross, we can almost hear:

"I understand what it means to be condemned."
"I understand what it means to be abandoned."
"I know trauma
"I know shame"
"I know what sin feels like"
"I know how hard it is to forgive amidst torture."
"I know what it means to the outcast and to be hated."
"I know how it feels to be innocent yet still be convicted."

"I know what it feels like to be imperfect."
"I understand violation, torture, abuse, and shame."
"I understand being alone and in complete, utter, unbearable pain."
"I put aside my strength so I can become the weakest and absorb death."
"I put aside my reputation so that I may take the blame for you."

Ultimately, it is fair to say, *the dying Jesus becomes the ultimate empath for humanity.*

In observing these possible messages, I hope you can feel the breath we are afforded from Jesus. Knowing a God that knows me and how I feel makes things….connected.

I've Fallen Down and I Need Your Help

In simple terms, the Cross is the story of how we all have chaos and disorder in our life. We either invite suffering into our lives or it comes into our life on its own. How we go about addressing our failures, shortcomings, and sin is worth sorting out. For the record, I am not a proponent of sin management because of the meanings from the Cross and it flies in the face of grace and forgiveness. I am, however, a proponent of being mindful to align our lives with truth—into the true self as Christ says we are. Simply put, I am a proponent of keeping life in order. Sin is disorder. What's essential about the Cross is that by Jesus taking up His Cross and becoming sin, he sends a message to the world, saying, "The power of all this sin is gone. So when you fall, know that I hold you tightly in my love, as you stand up and sort out your life." For those who follow Christ, the consequences of our failures are immediate, not eternal, all because of what Jesus did on the Cross.

And so we fall down. Down is where we often miss the most opportunistic moments of our life. As Richard Rohr eloquently writes in *The Universal Christ*: "I do not need to deny my own failures, and can recognize that even my mistakes are the truest and most surprising path to love." (Rohr, 2019) Whether in small ways, moderate ways, and sometimes even big ways, we all fall. What astonishes me, however, is when we do "fall down" we are often utterly surprised and even dismayed that it occurred. "What? Me? I did that? Unbelievable!" It's kind of comical because it's such a denial of our own nature. As humans, we are hardwired to fall. Like hiking or trail running, when we stumble and fall, we look back and see the root surging through the surface. We are surprised because we did not see it, but now we do. We shake our heads, evaluate the damage, and are more on the lookout for any more "roots."

Such it is in other places we fall down: relationships with companions, substances, food, work, and in other areas in which we display destructive behavioral patterns. We act surprised for myriad reasons: we didn't think it could happen And so we fall down. Down is where we often miss the most opportunistic moments of our life. Whether in small ways, moderate ways, and sometimes even big ways, we all fall. What astonishes me, however, is when we do "fall down" we are often utterly surprised and even dismayed that it occurred. "What? Me? I did that? Unbelievable!" Because it's such a denial of our own nature. As humans, we are hardwired to fall. Like hiking or trail running, when we stumble and fall, we look back and see the root surging through the surface. We are surprised because we did not see it, but now we do. We shake our heads, evaluate the damage, and are more on the lookout for any more "roots." Such is the case in other places we fall: relationships with companions, substances, food, work, and in other areas in which we display destructive behavioral patterns. We act surprised for myriad reasons: we didn't think it could happen to us, we didn't think we'd get caught, we didn't think we'd get addicted, we didn't think it went too far… and we get surprised by our own sinister behavior. Denial has special blinders causing us to be modern-day Neanderthals.

Of course, I've fallen down many times in my life—physically, morally, emotionally, and often mentally. Specifically, I recall a falling down as a young boy. I fell from my motocross bicycle during a day of mountain bike jumping, and when I fell, my immediate reaction was to jump up and run. It was sheer instinct. It was my mind trying to figure out if my body was really injured.

When we fall down, it's our instinct to just get up and carry on with life. But this is the real tragedy—falling and not taking the time to learn. As Richard Rohr eloquently illustrates in his classic book *Falling Upward*, "do not pardon your sins too quickly for you will miss out on the lessons they want to teach you and will have to relearn them." (Rohr,2011) This is such a spot-on observation because he is referring to the same lesson from Jesus' story about the house with unclean spirits. If you don't clean your house thoroughly of unclean spirits they will just come back again. We must take the time and the space to sort out for ourselves what our fall meant. Why did it occur?

I have learned it's often a lonely obstacle in life to find a safe place to heal from our falls. If we don't have that friend, confidant, mentor, etc., then life is a lonely place to not sort out such things. Mentorship, pastoral care, community, or therapy is the place where we get to come into a safe, controlled, and accepting place to sit with our fallings/sins/dilemmas and carefully sort them out and listen to the message we need to learn. All the while, we try to keep the self-judgment, condemnation, and guilt aside so we can see what helped create the fall or patterned behavior. We do this to heal from the hurt the fall created. We do this to come to terms with why we do what we do.

If we can just take the time to learn, and discover ourselves after the fall, we learn valuable insights about ourselves and others and even God. Falling down is designed that way. Yes, we learn why we do what we do and new strategies to cope with life differently, but more importantly, we have opportunities to experience levels of grace and forgiveness that transform us for the rest of our lives.

So, we go and get "help". We see a counselor or talk to our pastor, friend or mentor, and we start to address problems. We look at how to apply our Christian faith. And then the topic of sin arises. Sin—and all that entails. Yes, it's an easy correlation—our fall is either labeled as sin or sin caused our fall. Now, here is where, in my experience, things can get a little problematic. How the church has handled and viewed sin makes all the difference in how people practice their faith, worship, pray, and know God. Therefore, if we don't have a workable and functional understanding of the most unprecedented, ultimate, iconic, act known to man—the Crucifixion, then we miss out on the gift of His sacrifice.

I know, you would think most Christians could tell you what happened on the Cross. But they generally give a basic meaning that I find lacking. They say Jesus died on the Cross to forgive our sins and pay the penalty of sin for us. But there is more to it than that. I want to make some connections to other parts of the biblical story. But before I do, I want to go back and address why all this matters from a spiritual and mental health perspective.

To be clear, one of the purposes of the Cross is to give us a space to sort out our falling down without shame and self-condemnation. When we find ourselves in hurtful situations and reach out for help or start therapy, at some point in the healing process there is a run-in with the barbwire of shame and guilt, aching to find resolve. And the degree by which this gets addressed, I have noticed, depends on one's understanding of his or her relationship with God. What does He think about me? What does He think about what I've done or what I'm doing or what has happened to me? Further, what we think God's view is of broken lives and broken behaviors makes all the difference in how we get back up again. For instance, when we sin, if we believe we follow a harsh, judgmental, condemning God, guilt and shame are magnified. If we believe God is unable to understand our personal dilemmas, that He is a removed God, then we feel hopeless and alone. If we see God as all-controlling then God is to blame.

Our view of God matters. It affects how we "get up" (or don't "get up"), And how we recover from our hurts, our mistakes, our addictive patterns. How we view God and how we think God views us and our behaviors greatly impacts how we recover in life. So, how do you think God views you? Take a moment and ponder that. If we look closely at what was really happening at the Cross, we can learn what it's telling us, what God and His Son were accomplishing, and we can begin to hear the echo of the Cross a bit more clearly. We need to pay close attention to Jesus' final cry from the Cross. He says, "Father, into your hands I commit my spirit" (Luke 23:46 NASB2020) and "It is finished" (John 19:30 NASB 2020). Many a time we may have read that or seen it portrayed in movies or plays. But what does He mean by "It is finished" (*Mashalem* in the Aramaic)? Consider some of these meanings spoken and some non-spoken from the Cross.

Psychological Meanings Taught From the Cross

Here is what we can listen and learn from while we observe the Cross. When meeting with people in my clinical counseling work, these are the messages I point toward. Christ on the cross displays and models for us these major principles that we can mimic, absorb and align our lives by. Mostly, Christ gives us the modeling of combating suffering.

Brief descriptions of psychological meanings and lessons from the Cross:

Falling is essential. Imperfect beings produce imperfect behavior. Falling in the simplest definition, like sin, is missing the mark of what is right and good. Falling is essential so it can be our teacher of insight and growth. If we go about falling down with responsibility it brings about meaning. Falling reminds us we need saving.

Suffering has meaning: Throughout this whole chapter, suffering seems to be the central context. But I want to simply say that the Cross exemplifies how we all might take on suffering and bear our own cross in life. Jesus takes on the cross with humility and powerful surrender. He keeps his gaze on the Father and takes on responsibility for himself and the whole. The antidote to suffering is responsibility and fixating on God, love, and the highest good. Taking responsibility for our situations in life is what sustains the long walk of suffering. Amidst living and dying meaning requires Responsibility. There is evil and benevolence and there needs to be a stance of responsibility. The reason is, that when we cannot *own* our lives, the blessings, and the tragedy, we are then only victims of life and disconnected from the whole story.

Christ The Great Empath: Rejection, abuse, and trauma mocked, outsider, villainized, falsely accused. By Jesus, God in the form of man, subjecting Himself to being human and ultimately crucified, displays that He knows all the forms of pain and suffering in its ultimate degree. Therefore, He empathizes with us, and shows how we might respond to pain and suffering. There is a psychological reprieve when we acknowledge a God who can empathize with our pain. And can show us how to respond to that suffering. This brings up the next meaning. Forgiveness.

Forgiveness: A breath that exists as the antidote to hate, fear, and pain. In His final hours, dying in front of his family, and followers, his accusers and abusers, Jesus cries out, "forgive them, they no not what they do." Jesus did not allow tragedy or pain to be his escape from the moment. He instead chose to forgive his torturers and accusers. In the most painful moment physically and emotionally Jesus reaches for the highest road, dignity. As described by Fr Rohr, "In forgiveness, we live up to our truest dignity. We operate by a power not our own."

I realize the possible temptation for Jesus on the Cross, and how at the start of his ministry, he was in another physically agonizing position in the desert. At the end of himself he chooses to live by a power not of his own,

His Father's word, and by His Father's Power. At the end of His ministry, Jesus offered the opportunity to be the victim of betrayal and abuse and chose to forgive. The ultimate forgiveness to forgive all humankind's sins. It's forgiveness that makes us better people. We learn, that forgiving others not only helps our soul (more in the Forgiveness chapter) but it helps make others better, acknowledging their better parts in light of their 'falling down' toward us.

Weakness is Power: What is real power? Power is a force in the world that drives most anything, and everything. Much of our modern culture is fueled by power structures in corporate business or the pursuit of financial 'security'. There are many faces and forms of power that we come upon social, physical, status, financial, emotional, and psychological powers. Power is often negotiated in our most intimate and even casual relationships. It's a force that can build as easy as it can destroy.

We all have our relationship with power in some form or another. Power is associated with our core need for certainty/ security. But what is real power anyway? I would present that there are 2 kinds of power; true and false power. It is sought after in many ways: money, sexual allure and attraction, positions of authority in business and other organizations, knowledge, degrees, possessions, relational alignments etc. Power sought out in these methods, rarely allows us to find ultimate fulfillment. If anything, pursuing power in these manners ultimately leaves us empty and yearning for more; as if too much is not enough.

Observing the cross we observe power by another means. Vulnerability. Vulnerability unearths for us an undeniable power. Vulnerability is what attracts us more to others than sheer/overt power and strength. Sheer force is impressive and a face of power. Yet, I have always been enthralled with this concept of finding strength in perceived acts/attributes of weakness. Acts of love, grace, mercy, forgiveness manifest a certain quiet force of power that transforms individuals and communities, more than wealth, dominance, excess or force. "Most gladly, therefore, I will rather boast about my weaknesses, so that the power of Christ may dwell in me. Therefore, I delight in my weaknesses… on behalf of Christ for when I am weak, then I am strong." (2 Corinthians 12:9-10).

A dying Jesus on the cross could easily lend us to viewing the ultimate act of helplessness. Rather, in a closer look, we can peel back the layers of the scene; blood, torn flesh, pierced limbs and appendages. As we follow the full story line, we discover this is the ultimate perfect human (God in human flesh) who was not particularly guilty of any "crime" willingly offering up his own life for the betterment of the whole. He put aside his supernatural ability to rescue himself. Resulting in his death or yet sacrifice (weakness) becoming profoundly powerful that it echoed, and keeps echoing through the gates of time; 100, 1000, 2000 years and counting. By the apostle Paul realizing his 'weakness, or thorn' was not to be removed it caused him to be dependent upon God and not his own strength. His weakness became the thing that caused him to boast in his need for God and God's grace. Humility, vulnerability, true power.

Sacrifice Principle: *"Whoever strives to save his life will lose it, and whoever loses his life will keep it" (Luke 17:23 NASB 2020)* Jesus sums up the principle of sacrifice in that statement. It is paradoxical and true. You can't have your life in full if what you do is hold onto yourself, your gifts, and your offerings. You cannot obtain anything of value if it doesn't cost you something. As beings that seek out self-preservation, often the inclination to sacrifice is missed on us. It seems we have a reflex to protect ourselves, our egos, our comforts. This is manifested in so many ways: addictions to food, substance, and visuals. We preserve our intimate thoughts and feelings. We strive to promote ourselves and our needs. But what we see on the cross is the power of sacrifice; doing an act that puts aside self-preservation so that the other(s) can advance and thrive. Sacrifice is a principle/act that seems essential in our living that the Cross teaches. Jesus sacrificed Himself, putting aside His strength, His will and His innocence so that the rest of the "whole" (humankind) can have a relationship with God, be forgiven, and be innocent. His sacrifice benefitted the whole. This is a principle for us to integrate in life as we approach our own involvements in life i.e. Marriage, parenting, friendships, family, teams, work, and society as a whole.

Sometimes these situations we find ourselves in are asking us to sacrifice ourselves so that the rest of the whole/group can thrive. As the apostle Paul says, "Do nothing from selfish or empty conceit but with humility consider one another as more important than yourselves." (Philippians 2:3 NASB 2020). If we don't sacrifice, the situation/ group/ relationship can only remain as it is, stagnant and sometimes get worse. It seems to be a patterned principle that when things are sacrificed for something/someone else, the meaning and value increase. We usually cannot value something unless we sacrifice ourselves for it. Simply put, sacrifice adds meaning and value. And over time we see that the more we refuse to sacrifice for the whole, whatever you're a part of will diminish in meaning and value.

The Blood Stained Dirt: The cross provides this sacred space for us to sort out our falling down. I imagine there is blood spilling down his body, down the vertical beam, and onto the ground. And on the ground is a space of scarlet-stained dirt. And we get to, figuratively, sit there on the scarlet dirt, Jesus looking down upon us providing protection, mercy, empathy, love, companionship, forgiveness, vulnerability and acceptance. In that space He welcomes us to sit with him in His suffering, Him contending with our sin as we contend with ours.

And what is lacking in this moment is something very profoundly missing. In this scarlet blood stained dirt lacks all the guilt, and condemnation that I am so familiar with. So attached to my guilt and shame I almost think I need to have it around in this moment. But, no. That is what He is protecting me from. He Lords over me, on that rugged ugly despicable cross, as I am sitting in the dirt, protecting me from the shame. Here I see it is him condemned, willingly, intentionally. He cries, "Father forgive him, he really hasn't yet figured out and decided on some things. I accept the punishment. Father love Him as you love me."

So I sit there sorting out my moral and insidious failure/ sin. How did I get here? Why did I get here? And how can I never do this again? I look up. He is dying. He turns his gaze down at me, and the look in His eyes at me is devastatingly beautiful. Though He is dying, He is yet full of more life than I can take in. His eyes, pierce me. As if those eyes have seen everything and know everything ever done, spoken or thought.

His gaze holds me and my whole life in that moment. I cannot hear anything, I am lost and locked into His eyes. The strongest sense of Love I'll ever know. He loves and loved me so much in my worst moment. Not needing to say a word, his eyes shout, "I see your heart. I know your heart. Give it to me. I know what you do and did. And I Love you so much. Father adores you. I understand why and how this happened. I'll be your worst moment. Grab that blood-filled dirt. Get up! Go…and remember me, remember us. I will be taking your sin to hell with me and rise again into the Father's arms."

In the meantime, in the present and future, we get to sit at the foot of the cross and figure out who we are with Him and who I am with myself. See, when we understand who we are with Him (God, Jesus), in Him becomes a starting point. And this is how I see the Cross providing breath. It provides a space to sort out ourselves. Our behavior, our heart, our identity without the 'weight' from our failure, without the weight of 'sin'

Posture: The Cross teaches posture. When we look at Jesus on the cross, we see the posture of how we might live. We get to live with arms wide open, and vulnerable, and eyes for the vulnerable. Throughout His ministry and until the very end, Jesus was inclusive to all. He always invited and called everyone to a part of Him. He reached out to the less fortunate the lowly. We see the posture of Jesus is what made Him the most profound figure of all history. How we posture ourselves can take a lesson from Jesus. Our stance. Are you being open or exclusive? Do you reach toward the fortunate and favored in society or the lesser? Is our posture humble or self-promoting? Is our posture defensive and fearful or is it courageous vulnerability? These are some of the profound challenges from the cross and opportunities to arrange/align ourselves accordingly.

The power of meaning. At first glance, the Cross (crucifix) is often seen as a symbol of tragic sacrifice. Hopefully, as you are reading this, you are realizing there is an array of meanings coming from the cross. Another psychological lesson the cross offers is how we place meanings onto things in life. As discussed earlier the cross has ways of displaying counter-intuitive messages like, weakness equals real power, suffering and sacrifice bring meaning etc. What we can learn here is the act of Jesus to become the sin for the world and conquer the power of sin is a game changer. Sin or our failures in life do not have to define us in a shameful way because the Cross says, "You are forgiven and loved no matter what you do".

Instead of sin or failing to be the defining act, we get to fail and learn from it and grow. We get to find new meaning from our failures, meanings that produce hope and insight, not condemnation. We can take charge in life of what meaning we put on situations we find ourselves. There is usually more than one meaning we can put on something. It takes a little bit of work and reframing in ourselves to do that. The Cross offers space and grace for us to do so. Just for example, cancer. I have witnessed how the meaning of cancer has different faces.

My future father-in-law, because he passed before Marie and I got married, was diagnosed with cancer at a relatively young age. He was featured on a local news show as a special story, and he spoke of his cancer like this. "I was diagnosed with cancer a while ago, and I honestly tell you it is a gift! I was a man not very nice and took many things for granted. But now, I thank God every day I am alive and get to help people and be with my family, a true gift".

Another is how cancer is a curse. I have seen cancer represent the end for people causing sheer fear, bitterness and despair. Meaning, we get to seek out different meanings to put on life's situations. The Cross teaches us this principle very profoundly. What looks like the end of a religious movement, the end of the life of Jesus was only the beginning of the largest movement in human history. Meaning. I would like for you to reflect and see what needs a new meaning in your life.

An antidote to Shame: Shame is the cancer of the soul. It feels like it will never leave. The Cross teaches us that you are not alone nor the worst person to have ever lived. It means God became the worst and knows the shame you feel, but He being the ultimate good, has no shame for you because he became your shame. God loves you in light of your failure and sin. You are not a bad person, you are of the highest value because He laid His life down for you. He became our worst moment so we might live on in freedom of shame and guilt.

Further, Jesus helps us work out our brokenness by giving us a road to recovery. Whether that be addictions, impulsive mistakes, and any numerous kinds of destructive patterns we have developed and nurtured, Jesus helps resurrect us into His righteousness. "Therefore, we are ambassadors for Christ....He made Him who knew no sin to be sin in our behalf, so that *we might become the righteousness of God in Him.*" (2Corinthians 5:20-21 NASB 2020) Turning shame into glory!

Vertical & Horizontal Horizons (the symbol) The Cross is like a life code of ultimate good and ultimate wrong. As humans, we need a reference point, the borders. We look to references so we can measure ourselves, and gauge our bearings. The cross exemplifies the ultimate sin. As scripture describes "He made Him who knew no sin to be sin in our behalf" (2 Corinthians 5:21 NASB). The ultimate Love, to live well horizontally, the vertical relationship needs to be understood.

The cross can be a symbol for us in the following manner. Vertically: the connected road from our heart to our head usually requires work and sometimes repair. Often we can get disconnected between our heart and mind and that leads to troubles. When the heart hurts, our mind needs to learn how to talk to it with kindness and forgiveness.

When our mind is lost, our heart lets us know the meaning of it all. And when our hearts and minds are well, we can horizontally treat the world around us in a better manner. In the bigger picture, when we realize of what Jesus did on the Cross our vertical relationship with God is at peace. We get to learn about our identity with God through Christ. We are fueled by our vertical relationship with God. We have a secure relationship with God because of the work on the Cross by Jesus. And because of what Jesus has taught us and shown us, we can live horizontally (toward others) in a more loving and graceful manner. In addition, as we live out the gospel here on earth, in the Body of Christ, we share the gospel with one another and the world.

The other way the cross is a breath for us is how to live in the *tension* between the vertical life and horizontal life. Vertically we live in Christ, a relationship with

God through Jesus because of sacrifice. We live horizontally with and toward others through the way of the cross. Vertically, we get to have communication with the Father. We can go to Him at any and every time. Vertically we learn about our identity in Christ. We are given direct access to God the Father. The Vertical relationship we have is the most important one of our life. It is our connection to the 'eternal'. And our vertical relationship is where we are empowered by knowledge, wisdom, love and grace of God.

If we take the cross as symbol, we can learn from this symbol. A part I want to bring our attention toward right now, is the center where the vertical beam meets the horizontal beam; where profound tension lives. Right there at the cross section of horizontal and vertical, it can represent where the spirit and flesh combine. And in that cross section lives the tension and chaos of those two forces we are bound by.

Graphically the apostle Paul writes about this in the letter to the Galatians. Paul describes that the flesh and spirit war against one another. Further, there are some theological interpretations from the original language that describe it as 'lust after one another' to do the work as the other; lusting for prominence in us. Fascinating idea. Nonetheless, the horizontal and vertical is the place on the cross we are connected by. And we spend our life figuring out how we live in the tension of both. The horizontal, described here as the way of the cross is our day to day living amongst God's creation. The horizontal represents our life in the flesh. In horizontal living we get to learn how we love others, and practice the way of Jesus. While being fueled vertically, we can live the horizontal life with hope. We can contend with suffering, trials and adversity. We can love others with compassion and grace. Our vertical life is fed by God, through the Spirit, because of Jesus, so we can live powerfully in the 'horizontal'.

This is the code of the cross: Falling is essential+Suffering has meaning+Christ the Great Empath+Forgiveness+Weakness is Power+Sacrifice Principle+Blood Stained Lives+Posture+Power in Meaning+Antidote to shame+Vertical Horizontal.

MASHALEM "IT IS FINISHED" PART II

Theology of The Cross
Scriptural Review
&
Definition of Sin

OUR SIN CAN take our breath away. Whatever the detail is of any of our sins, it tends to suck oxygen out of our life. One of the biggest components of the Christian faith, and most all religions, is the concept of "sin". The understanding of "sin" and what it is and how it's addressed, is arguably one of the most determinant factors in how any individual, group, church, denomination, or religion practices its beliefs. Theology of sin is one of those defining doctrines for churches. The practice of understanding God some would argue, is centered upon their understanding of "sin". In my opinion, if Grace and forgiveness received as much press as sin, I imagine the church would find itself to be more of a light to the world.

There are two major theological positions about the cross. One is the Penal Substitution theology and the other is Cristus Victor position. Simply put, the Penal Substitution theology frames the cross as Jesus being the sacrificial lamb to take the punishment for man so satisfy God's need for atonement of mankind's sin. Jesus taking the punishment, and penalty for sin in place of us. This is very prominent in many Christian denominations, churches. Cristus Victor came from the writings of Gustaf Aulén in 1931. Aulen reports how Cristus Victor theology is what was most taught in the first 1000 years by early church fathers from Irenaeus to John of Damascus. To mention only the most important names Origen, Athanasius, Basil the Great, Gregory of Nyssa, Gregory of Nazianzus, and John Chrysostom. The Christus Victor view was also dominant among the Latin Fathers of the Patristic period including Ambrose, Augustine, Leo the Great, and Gregory the Great. Cristus Victor is the viewpoint that God defeated death and its reign of sin by Jesus going to the Cross. Jesus and God together kill death so mankind can be eternally free.

It has been my observation, being in the church for over 40 years, some of its members/leaders as being sin police and moral dictators. Feverishly trying to point out, and proclaim all the sins of their brothers and sisters in Christ, or in the world. Or teaching the doctrines of sin management by indoctrinating congregations with hyper importance of moral codes, behavioral compliances are the road to becoming righteous. Positioning themselves as moral dictators, "do good and don't sin or else" kind of messaging. All the while, this just enforces a kind of empowerment to sin that we do not need to be burdened by, and shamed by. It has created an empowerment of sin where we are in charge of managing it and behaviorally trying to address the dilemma of sin. And living under the condemnation of sin is what living under the Law was like for mankind.

What is sin exactly? There a several ways to define it. One of the common words used in the First Testament is "harmatia". Harmatia is used hundreds (over 270) times in scripture meaning: to miss the mark, to error and be mistaken, to be without a share, to wander from the path of uprightness, to do wrong, to wander from the Law of God, to violate God's law. What doesn't get observed enough, however, is how the word for sin shows up often as a noun and verb. Most of the time in our church world, sin is mostly viewed as an action or behavior. And that is accurate. But it is also important to understand it is a noun, a place, or state. It is one thing to "do" a sin and it's another thing to be "in sin".

Being in a state of sin is only when someone is not in a relationship with God through Christ. The unbeliever can be said to be in a state of sin. Once someone has recognized Jesus as their Messiah, they are "in" the Christ and no longer "in" sin. That is important because where you live or reside makes up a lot of your identity. Living "in" sin one can accurately be called sinners as Paul often describes sinners as non-believers and believers as 'believers and saints and the righteousness of God". Therefore, sin is the state and act of missing the mark, not having a share in God, and violating God's law (way).

The words of Jesus while on the cross, have echoed for over 2000 years. Mashalem. "It Is Finished!" Again, what do you suppose Jesus meant by that utterance? What is "finished" is the power of that lives within the sin. Jesus took on the burden of sin, to kill the power of sin, by becoming sin and overcoming it by his resurrection. No more will mankind have to 'fix' their sin. Instead, Jesus kills the power of sin by taking it on, being the sacrifice, so that there is eternal access to God regardless of our actions and deeds. Jesus takes away the separation sin creates in the world and between mankind and God. Jesus on the Cross and his walking out of his own tomb conquered the power of death and sin. The power of sin, the shame from sin, is finished!

Sin can be described simply as us 'missing the mark' in life, that which is done wrong, an offense, a violation of the divine law in thought or act. Whether one is a believer in God/Jesus or not, all can relate to the idea of sin. It is when we act out inappropriately or miss the mark that our lives become disordered, even chaotic. And further, it is because of that sin our inner world becomes troubled with regret, guilt, shame, and fear. And as those feelings remain harbored in us, the soul gets depressed and hopeless. What tends to occur, is our souls get so weighted down by these feelings, and the memories begin to interfere with our self-image and how we relate to others. Sin provides this sense of separateness between ourselves and what we know is our better self. I think this is what shame causes in us. Shame says we are not good. It is a very defining state and feeling. It is oh-so-very powerful. As we carry that horrid feeling in us, it is no wonder as we continue on in life, this shame/sin in us also compromises us in our future efforts in living. In our relationships, in our work, and in how we take care of ourselves.

This is exemplified throughout the First Testament. How God's people (Israel) fail to measure up to the law, and those who think they have mastered the law consequently become blinded by self-righteousness. Enough bloodshed of 'clean' animals was not going to be enough to keep mankind 'clean'. What wound up happening is that the law, though holy, could not fulfill God's intent for man to live righteously, to hit the mark. This sort of arrangement caused catastrophic results on a nation and its people.

The power and meaning of sin only seemed to wreck one's soul. And even the hot pursuit of trying to follow a highly moralistic life has its own way of creating some kind of subtle havoc on one's mental health. Something needed to be done about how man can live in an arrangement with God that was not entangled in a system set up for failure. As it is articulated in Paul's letter to the Corinthians, he describes how God and Jesus decided to overcome death/sin by Jesus becoming the ultimate and final sacrifice for all of mankind's sin. "The sting of death is sin, and the power of sin is the law, but thanks be to God who gives us the victory through our Lord Jesus Christ" (1 Corinthians 15:56 NASB 2020). Though Jesus lived the perfect life; the life we were supposed to live and yet he was crucified. It is beautifully said and sums up the work on the cross by Jesus as said by the apostle Paul,. "For our sake he made him to be sin who knew no sin, so that in Him we might become the righteousness of God. (2 Corinthians 5:21 NASB 2020).

One of the best discourses I have been presented with is by my dear friend, and spiritual mentor, Jim Griffin. I won't restate the whole essay, but here are the excerpts that sum up this topic of sin.

Pastor Griffin Discourse

Whether used in a noun or verb sense we have been taught the action nature of the word. The concepts of being "born in sin" or existing in a state of disconnect from God quickly lose their significance as all manner of discussions arise surrounding the action of sin and the remedy thereof. Concepts of transgression, violation, offense, missing the mark, age of accountability, and trespass all reflect the behavioral nature of sin in both the child and the adult.

In contrast, when we look at the definition of sin from the Greek lexicons we see the primary definition being reflective of a state or condition whose remedy is not behaviorally addressed. To be without a share in, to have no part in, to be without the necessary ingredient for communion with God is a condition only remedied by the One who dispenses the share, the One who holds and controls that thing we lack

Sin is primarily a condition, not a behavior. The very definition from the language of the NT in both noun and verb forms shows us SIN is a condition of being without a share, having no part in.

This is further illuminated when we consider the consequences of the condition in which we exist. Having no share, no part in the design to which we were created sets the stage for all manner of compensatory behaviors and outcomes; the secondary definitions of SIN, and indeed the symptoms of the condition.

> *Christ's plan of redemption addresses the condition, the cause, and in doing so brings address to the symptoms and outcomes of sin. We must look the order of this plan to fully understand the incredible blessing that is the Grace of God*
>
> *Most theology that I have experience, Christian and otherwise, are focused on a redress(fix) of the symptoms and outcomes of sin and miss the true beauty of Grace wherein redemption is completed by addressing the condition and cause of sin. When the first approach is taken, the exercise is always one of futility because the address is centered on our behavior, the things we do or don't do to a state of rightness. (Griffin 2000)*

Pastor Jim presents to us the distinction of sin as a state/condition and a behavior. He makes the point that the address of sin should probably first come from treating the condition which was done by Jesus' act on the cross resulting in Grace. God resolves sin, not our behavior. Further, addressing the internal alignment of that act of Grace is our path to order. He made a good point here that all too often we get caught in the management of behavior to address behavior. Not having a share in was insightful. Not being "in Christ" is not having a share. Being "in Christ" we have a share. Seeing sin as a "state" is important. Not being in that state is completed by what Jesus did on the cross. So the point of this theological research is for us to start to break down what sin "is" and is not. Looking at sin as a state, as a condition, and a behavior. Naturally, due to the nature of this condition, it has been man's striving to resolve such a thing. Here is a simple layout for this:

Fear attachment:
Sin Theology Case 1: If I sin, then I am not ok with God.
Sin Theology Case 2: If I stop my sin, I will be ok with God.
Sin Theology Case 3: If I sin, I am a sinner
Sin Theology Case 4: If I don't sin then I am not a sinner
Sin Theology Case 5: If I sin, God cannot use me.

Secure attachment:
Grace Theology Case 1: If I sin, I am still ok with God
Grace Theology Case 2: If I stop my sin, I am still ok with God and with others
Grace Theology Case 3: If I sin, I am not a sinner and still a saint
Grace Theology Case 4: If I don't sin then I am a saint walking in my identity and the fruit of Spirit
Grace Theology Case 5: If I sin, God can and will still use me

Sin Management vs Living by Your Identity

The non-productive address to the sin dilemma? Sin management. There are various ways by which we individuals, church and institutions make the attempt to manage ones sin, or our behaviors. It's such an anxiety-ridden march that we do this. This is sort of in our broken fleshly DNA to think we can make ourselves righteous before God. In general, sin management is different than living in accordance with one's identity and true self in Christ. It is different than making conscious decisions to live a life of order and morality. As the apostle Paul writes in his letter to the church in Ephesians, "We are created to do good works".

Sin management first comes from the internal motive of fear of God, not the healthy "awe" type fear of God, but fear of God punishing you and not feeling good about you kind of fear, and the guilt that you did something or thought something 'unholy', 'evil' or 'carnal', or 'sinful'. Much of sin management comes from a legalistic theological framework as laid out by Pastor Griffin in cases 1-5. Sin management is when we act as police toward our behaviors through fear and in insecure attachment to God. Sin management is also something manifested from having a distorted image of your identity in Jesus Christ.

The problem with our response to sin is our compulsion of sin management. The allure of sin management is that it entices our appetite for control and progression and the thirst for us to earn our way into good graces with the eternal. Man, since the beginning of time it seems, thirsts to perform his worth and value. We have strong ties to earning our way into most everything.

The healthy address to this dilemma is how we answer am I a Saint or a Sinner? A *healthy secure attachment to God* would follow the belief that since the act on the Cross resolved the power of sin, once and for all, then one believes in the Christ is secure within the Christ. . The apostle Paul writes we are "sealed in Him by the Spirit", and "Saved by grace and not of your works" (Eph 2:8-9 NASB2020). And once one has aligned/believed/accepted Christ, they are no longer in a state of sin and are now positioned and have a 'share in Christ'. Further, the believer is described in great detail, in many ways by the Apostle Paul who declares, "We are his righteousness". (2 Corinth5 NASB2020). He again proclaims "We are his inheritance; adopted by and in him forgiven, redeemed, blameless". (Ephesians 1 NASB 2020).

There is a distinction in scripture when the apostles are discussing sinners, they are ones referred to as 'not believing'. And the ones who believe are "saints". Common Christian verbiage is 'ah we are all sinners, just saved by grace". But that's an oxymoron. It is equal to saying 'We are nonbelievers saved by grace'. Saying we 'were sinners/non-believers saved by grace' actually makes sense.

Now do we sin? Yes. And when we sin our consequence is not eternal. Rather, our consequence of sin usually is the chaos we create between ourselves and others. In addition, the chaos we cause internally, creates anxiety and sadness for the things we commit. So when we 'sin' / fall we are not in a state of sin yet we are in Christ still.

I urge you to try and do a phrase count in the New Testament. Dozens of times we read the believer is "in Christ". Count how many times this comes up in the New Testament. Being "in Christ" exposes we cannot be in 2 places at once. Being "in harmatia sin" was prior to knowing Jesus. Once one believes by faith, they are as Paul says, "Therefore if anyone is in Christ, this person is a new creation." You do not lose your adoption by Christ through your actions. Our actions are not stronger than the Cross. Therefore, it is more accurate to come to a more secure position that through and by His grace and act on the Cross, we are forever Saints, no longer sinners. The *power of sin* is no more because "MASHALEM".

The correction is in our understanding. Scripture defines anyone who is not "in" Christ or has not come to the salvation of Jesus Christ is in a state of sin; not taking share in Him. A sinner is not taking part of Christ. Anyone who accepts Jesus as Lord and Savior is partaking in Christ and is "in" Christ. Therefore, if someone is "In" Christ, how can they be "in" sin? Again, we cannot be in 2 states at once. So when a believer "in" Christ, commits a "sin", it is an act of chaos with what a believer is otherwise equipped to do. IT is an act that will most likely create an immediate consequential situation; not an eternal one. It can also create a momentary distraction of focus from the spiritual to the flesh. The sin act does not, however, create a separation from them to God. It does not put one in judgment with God. It is an action that won't damn you as much as a holy act won't save you. The sinful act will however potentially create some problematic circumstances in one's life that can be excruciatingly painful and messy. And one has to contend with those outcomes from 'sinful' actions. The outcome of "mashalem" is that the power of sin has been taken by the spilling of the blood of Jesus.

So what is the big idea here? Why am I diving into this topic, as a Christian therapist? Well, I think to know ourselves, I think we need to know where we came from who we became, and how we know Him. Further, what do we do with Jesus and the crucifixion? How we know the meaning of this, shapes how we know and understand God. Further, how we know the message of God shapes how we know ourselves and treat others.

Now we get into our own psychology and philosophy of life. The crucifixion shapes and helps contextualize my shame. The crucifixion helps me be reminded that I get to be an inclusive, arms-wide-open, human toward others. The crucifixion displays a God spilling over His life (blood) so I may live forever. The crucifixion reminds me I too get to spill my life toward others so they can be comforted, loved, and lifted. The crucifixion, reminds me that I am loved by one who is much bigger than I. I am loved by one who understands pain, abandonment, shame and rejection. The crucifixion reminds me of me at my worst, yet I am loved. The crucifixion tells me that He waits there, hanging on, patiently in torture until I can be patient toward others. It says I am loved by one who knows me better than I. Jesus on the Cross is all I have; and all I have lives in me; and what lives in me changes me and changes the world. This is why I think the crucifixion is worth staring at for the rest of my life.

Again, the purpose here is twofold. Ultimately, glorifying God for the extension of His Grace is the essence of life. I hope to bring some light on the topic that can be a stumbling block to some and create some unnecessary mental, and emotional havoc in life. The bottom line message is that sin no longer defines who we are as people. Sin is/should not be the focal point of the Christian believer life. As much as we are compelled, we are not called to spend our time on earth, managing our sin or the extreme denial of its force. Yet, I am not suggesting here that the spiritual path is the minimization or denial of sin, for it is real and it is damaging to all of our lives.

My point and question here is simply, how does one take a stance in life? Is it the mediation on "not" doing something? Our meditation is upon all things living. As Paul states, we are dead to sin; so why must we act as if it's alive and vital? When we focus on things that are full of life and positive energy, we stay in a better "order" of things. We get to chase life and things that are good, pure, loving, right, and humble; not abstaining from certain acts. Chase life, not sin.

The Final Messages from The Cross

God understands your worst moment

God knows and understands the experience of being exposed and ashamed

Someone greater than you shows how we rise above agony and cares for the other

God feels alone and betrayed

Someone greater than you is in absolute physical agony.

The most innocent person became the most shamed and won't blame a soul.

Someone greater than you became imperfect so you don't have to pretend to be

Someone greater than you is the outsider like you feel

Someone greater than you, looks up to you because he is the worst of all

Someone greater than you, was considered guilty by the State and Religious standards, so you don't have to feel right to anyone or anything.

Someone greater than you took on poverty so you don't have to seek the deception of wealth.

Someone greater than you was not liked, but hated, so you don't have to try so hard to be liked or loved by anybody.

Someone who lived perfectly was willing to become imperfect and wrong so you don't have to be perfect or right or idealize the so-called normal.

Someone so strong became weak so you don't have to pretend to be strong.

On His Back

The most innocent of all became the murderer, rapist, mass murderer, thief, liar, batterer, bully, God hater, the glutten, and the slot. He understands what it means to be the most wrong. His name is Jesus. He knows the weight of becoming each of these. The guilt is killing him.

On his back, He bore the burden of love for all He came in contact with. His back is where many hands laid their affection and assurance upon; "thank you Jesus". His back is what he leaned on when sitting with sinners and priests teaching forgiveness and peace. His back is where he picked up the adulterer and carried her to safety from condemnation. His back, where he carried the Lamb. His back is what helped him stand firm against the hypocrisy of priests and evil. His back is where he laid on, staring up at heaven talking to his father.

His back is laid bare, while he is strapped to a post, His hands gripping the post and rope for support, on his knees to brace the pending impact. The sun, beating on his back in the afternoon light. Whoooop! Smack!!! Rope, bone, glass, thistles, dig in, penetrate, raping his back, digging, sheer heat. Then, a tug and pull, tearing inches of skin away from the deep tissues. Whooop Smack!!! Dig, pull, yanking more skin from the tissues. Blood starts to spill down his back. Whoop, Smack!!!, glass, bone, thistles dig into the tissue and pull chunks of tissue from his back. And another, whip hits, and another.. 39 lashes! Pulling and tearing the skin off of his back. The adrenaline has nearly numbed his body. The back is not recognizable. Its blood red, pink tissues, and some skin remain from the back of my Messiah. He picks up his cross to the hill of Golgotha, carrying my sins with him.. And then it is his back that is pinned against the cross, exposed flesh pressing into the harsh wood. It is His back is where He carries me every day. Never letting me fall.

Prayer

Jesus, thank you. You have killed the sting of death and sin. You brought us together by your ultimate sacrifice. In my mind's eye, I sit here in your blood-stained dirt, as you humbly lord over me. Help me to live in your order and by your heart. Help me to love others boldly as you do. To be content with what I am and what I have. Help me to be tolerant of others, that I can feel safe when I feel threatened; to be full of spirit, to care about your thoughts of me, more than what others think of me. May humility be my strength not my proof of accomplishments. Lord, I thank you for loving me as I am, for not letting me go, you never let me go, ever. For forgiving my sin, then and now and forever. I am in you as you are in me. I love you. "Mashalem!"

Amen.

REFERENCES

"Switch on The Brain" – Dr. Caroline Leaf 2013 pg. 52,53
"David and Goliath" – Malcolm Gladwell 2013
"Things Hidden" – Richard Rohr 2008
"The Universal Christ" – Richard Rohr 2019
" Falling Upward" – Richard Rohr 2011
NASB New American Standard Bible 2020
Caponi, Paolo. 2014. "Andre Agassi, Open. An Autobiography (London, Harpercollins, 2009, 388 Pp. ISBN 978-000-728-1435)." *Altre Modernità*, no. 12 (November): 161–63. https://doi.org/10.13130/2035-7680/4483
Rohr, Richard. 2019. *The Universal Christ: How a Forgotten Reality Can Change Everything We See, Hope For, and Believe.* Convergent Books.
Gladwell, Malcolm. 2013. *David and Goliath: Underdogs, Misfits, and the Art of Battling Giants.* Little Brown & Company.
Rohr, Richard. 2007. *Things Hidden: Scripture as Spirituality.* Franciscan Media.
Lawler-Row, K. A., & Piferi, R. L. (2006). The forgiving personality: Describing a life well lived? *Personality and Individual Differences, 41*(6), 1009–1020.
*U2 (2000) All That You Can't Leave Behind; Island Records
2020. *The Wisdom Pattern: Order, Disorder, Reorder.*
Leaf, Caroline. 2015. Switch on Your Brain: The Key to Peak Happiness, Thinking, and Health. Baker Books.

Arthur Bennett, ed., *The Valley of Vision: A Collection of Puritan Prayers and Devotions* (Edinburgh: Banner of Truth Trust, 1975).

Printed in Great Britain
by Amazon